THIS BOOK BELONGS TO

START DATE

| MONTH | DAY | YEAR |

# YOUaremine

## A LENTEN STUDY OF ISAIAH

SHE READS TRUTH

*Nashville, Tennessee*

*"The house of my soul is too small for you to come to it. May it be enlarged by you. It is in ruins, restore it."*

ST. AUGUSTINE

English class was always my favorite. I can't be certain, but I bet it was either Mr. Ellis or Mrs. Melton who taught me what a paradox is: a seemingly contradictory statement that, upon further investigation, holds truth. We probably had to present a few examples, carefully written in cursive across wide-ruled paper.

The gospel is full of paradox. To die is to live (Galatians 2:19). To bow down is to be lifted up (Psalm 145:14). To be last is to be first (Matthew 20:16). And the paradoxes are not just abstract; some are very tangible. The God of all creation really did become human (Galatians 4:4). The divine really did put on flesh (John 1:14). Sinners are made righteous and untouchables are embraced (2 Corinthians 5:21, Matthew 8:3).

In the gospel of Jesus Christ, the judgment and destruction deserved are remedied by the love and mercy given.

St. Augustine famously said, "The house of my soul is too small for you to come to it. May it be enlarged by you. It is in ruins, restore it." There is a paradox here, too. The destroyed become the restored. The small becomes the spacious. The sinful heart that cannot approach the holy God is made spotless and drawn close. This is the good news.

We have a saying in the She Reads Truth office: "Lent is *long*." That may not be profound, but it's true. This season is long—in days and weeks, and in conviction and repentance. And this season is necessary; we are forgetful people, and we need reminders of what is true. Lent is a 7-week journey of remembering our need for a Savior, a need met only in Jesus Christ.

We look to the cross, and recall that obedience, mercy, and love held Christ there. We look to the tomb, and remember that compassion, holiness, and power broke the shackles of death, walking fully alive into the light of day. We look to God's Word, and find it filled with true promises, sealed by the impossible reality of Jesus, who became the sacrifice so that we could be redeemed.

The book of Isaiah is long, too—sixty-six chapters to be exact. Sixty-six chapters of sin and judgment, redemption and restoration. Sixty-six chapters of a generations-long love story, written by the one true God to His people, wayward and loved.

I can't wait for you to discover what God has for you here in this book. There are 49 days of Scripture readings, beautiful artwork from the talented Emily Jeffords (that's her painting *Hope Rising* featured on the cover), insightful study aids, Lenten hymns—even seven gluten-free recipes from the kitchen of Danielle Walker. But it is all here to adorn one neon sign of a message: God is calling you to a life of restoration, accomplished through the work and power of Jesus Christ. Everything else plays second fiddle to this one true and glorious paradox: You are a sinner, and in Christ, you are redeemed. You are His.

*Amanda*

Amanda Bible Williams
EDITOR-IN-CHIEF

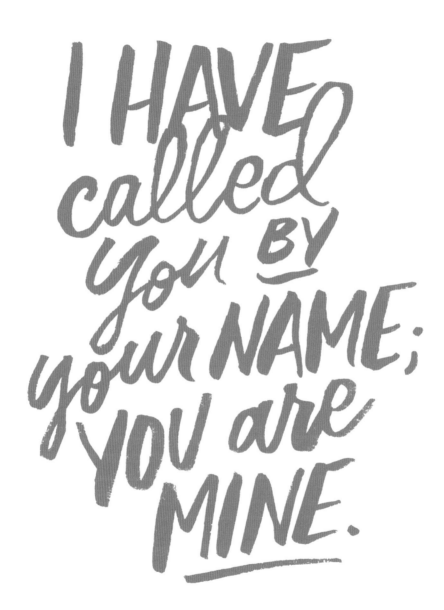

I HAVE called you BY your NAME; you are MINE.

KEY VERSE

*Now this is what the LORD says — the One who created you, Jacob, and the One who formed you, Israel — "Do not fear, for I have redeemed you; I have called you by your name; you are Mine." –ISAIAH 43:1*

ON THE TIMELINE:

Isaiah 6:1 records that Isaiah received his prophetic call in the last year of Uzziah's reign over Judah (about 742 B.C.), and Isaiah 37:38 suggests that he lived until the death of Sennacherib (681 B.C.). The events in Isaiah occur between those dates, around the time when the kingdom of Israel was taken into captivity by Assyria (722 B.C.).

A LITTLE BACKGROUND:

The book of Isaiah presents itself as the writing of Isaiah, son of Amoz. Not much is known about Isaiah apart from his prophecy. The superscription (an introductory element common to books of prophecy) in 1:1 dates Isaiah's prophetic activity as covering all or part of the reigns of four kings of Judah: Uzziah (783–742 B.C.), Jotham (742–735 B.C.), Ahaz (735–716 B.C.), and Hezekiah (716–686 B.C.).

The events prophesied extended beyond the eighth century B.C., through the rest of the OT period and beyond. Many New Testament authors cited prophecies from Isaiah as finding fulfillment in the events surrounding Jesus Christ.

MESSAGE & PURPOSE:

Isaiah's message to the nation of Judah is a straightforward one:

- Isaiah accused God's people of sin and rebellion against the One who made and redeemed them.

- He instructed them to turn from sin to obedience.

- He announced God's just judgment on them because of their sin.

- God revealed His future restoration of the people—the faithful remnant that survived the judgment. This restoration included both judgment on the nations (chapters 13–23) and a future turning of the nations to God (2:1-4).

The first part of the book of Isaiah (chapters 1–39) emphasizes sin, the call to repentance, and judgment. The second part (chapters 40–66) emphasizes the hope of restoration as revealed by God and foretold by the prophet.

---

**Give Thanks for the Book of Isaiah:**

Many readers are drawn to Isaiah for the passages describing a future anointed king, or Messiah (9:1-7; 11:1-9), and those describing the Suffering Servant (42:1-9; 49:1-6; 50:4-6; 52:13–53:12). But a full reading of Isaiah truly enriches our understanding of how these prophecies and more are indeed fulfilled in Jesus Christ. He is the Messiah; He is the Suffering Servant.

## HOW TO STUDY WITH THE ONLINE COMMUNITY

For added community and conversation, join us in the **Lent 2017: You Are Mine** reading plan on the She Reads Truth app or on SheReadsTruth.com—where women from Toledo to Thailand will be reading along with you!

**Have a "He" in your life**—a brother, father, husband, friend? Invite him to join you by visiting HeReadsTruth.com or the He Reads Truth app, or by picking up the guy version of this book at ShopHeReadsTruth.com.

She Reads Truth is a community of women dedicated to reading the Word of God every day. The Bible is living and active, breathed out by God, and we confidently hold it higher than anything we can do or say. This book focuses primarily on Scripture with helpful elements throughout.

*This study begins on Monday, **February 27**. The first day of Lent is Wednesday (Day 3 of the study), but we've provided two days of introduction to get you settled in.*

**GRACE DAY**

Each Grace Day includes a recipe and is designed to give you time to catch up on your reading, pray, and rest in the presence of the Lord.

**WEEKLY TRUTH**

This day is set aside for weekly Scripture memorization.

**SCRIPTURE READING**

This study book includes the complete text of Isaiah, plus supplementary passages for fuller context, as well as Gospel readings for Holy Week.

**JOURNALING SPACE**

Each daily reading includes space for notes, personal reflections, and prayers.

# table of CONTENTS

*Emily Jeffords, Morning Song, 2016, oil, 22x36, Private Collection*

"The book of Isaiah provides us with the most comprehensive prophetic picture of Jesus Christ in the entire Old Testament. It includes the full scope of His life: the announcement of His coming (Isaiah 40:3–5), His virgin birth (7:14), His proclamation of the good news (61:1), His sacrificial death (52:13–53:12), and His return to claim His own (60:2–3). Because of these and numerous other christological texts in Isaiah, the book stands as a testament of hope in the Lord, the One who saves His people from themselves."

CHARLES SWINDOLL

# What makes the book of Isaiah so unique?

**How does this book fit with the rest of the Bible?**

/ 1  **Isaiah reads like a microcosm of the whole Bible.** It walks through our rebellion against God, the promise of His coming judgment, and the assurance of a Savior.

/ 2  **Isaiah is quoted over 65 times in the New Testament**—more than any other prophet. He is also mentioned by name in the Old Testament over 20 times.

/ 3  **Isaiah prophesied through the reign of four kings:**
Uzziah (790-739 B.C.)
Jotham (739-731 B.C.)
Ahaz (731-715 B.C.)
Hezekiah (715-686 B.C.)

**WHO WAS ISAIAH?**

/ Isaiah was a contemporary of the prophets Jonah, Amos, Hosea, and Micah.

/ Isaiah appears to have been married to a woman whom he calls "the prophetess" (Isaiah 8:3).

/ Isaiah was likely a young man when he began this prophetic book, and he died when he was between 70-80 years old (c. 680 B.C.). He was an active prophet for around 60 years, using that entire duration to call Israel back to God.

**WHAT KIND OF PROPHET WAS HE?**

/ Isaiah's name means "The Lord Saves," a fitting summary of his prophetic message.

/ The word "salvation" appears nearly 30 times in the book of Isaiah, but only about 10 times by all the other prophets combined.

/ Isaiah features an uncommonly extensive vocabulary—over 2,100 unique words, as compared to around 1,500 in Ezekiel and Jeremiah.

/ Isaiah and other prophets were called "seers." They had visions. They saw their prophecies (Isaiah 1:1, 6:1; 2 Kings 6:17).

# *We Are His:*
# *A Lenten Introduction*

/ WEEK ONE

**During Lent, Christians traditionally meditate on Scriptures that point us to the life, death, and resurrection of Jesus Christ. When we see our desperate need for salvation through the lens of a cross and an empty tomb, we are reminded that nothing we cling to for security outside of Christ Himself can offer us any real or lasting hope.**

Isaiah's original audience, in the 8th century B.C., was made up of people in the process of losing their homeland. They wondered what God's solution would be, and if He even had one. Isaiah was written during a season of cultural and political unrest in Judah. Their good and steady king, Uzziah, died just as the opposing armies of Assyria chose Judah as their next nation to conquer. As the people of Judah waited and worried, Assyria subdued them and carried them off into exile.

Whatever hope God's people had put in their homeland was gone. All they had left to appeal to was the God of their fathers. All they could hope for was that God would intervene and save them. Lent reminds us that this salvation is all any of us can hope for, even as this season declares that Hope has come.

One of the most profound and beautiful qualities of Isaiah is how filled it is with references to the coming Savior of the world. Isaiah, more than any other book in the Old Testament, describes the coming of Christ in great detail. This prophet tells us about the One born of a virgin, on whom the Lord would lay the iniquity of us all. This Suffering Servant would be our Mighty God, Everlasting Father, and Prince of Peace, and by His wounds we shall be healed. He has called us by name; we are His (Isaiah 43:1).

During this Lent study, we will make our way through the message of restoration in the book of Isaiah. During the final week, we will also read Scripture passages from the Gospels that correspond with the events of Holy Week. Through Isaiah we will look ahead to the Savior, and through the Gospels we will look back on the salvation that is given to us in Jesus.

May your time in Isaiah cause you to worship the risen Christ.

## ACTS 8:26-40

### THE CONVERSION OF THE ETHIOPIAN OFFICIAL

²⁶ An angel of the Lord spoke to Philip: "Get up and go south to the road that goes down from Jerusalem to Gaza." (This is the desert road.) ²⁷ So he got up and went. There was an Ethiopian man, a eunuch and high official of Candace, queen of the Ethiopians, who was in charge of her entire treasury. He had come to worship in Jerusalem ²⁸ and was sitting in his chariot on his way home, reading the prophet Isaiah aloud.

²⁹ The Spirit told Philip, "Go and join that chariot."

³⁰ When Philip ran up to it, he heard him reading the prophet Isaiah, and said, "Do you understand what you're reading?"

³¹ "How can I," he said, "unless someone guides me?" So he invited Philip to come up and sit with him. ³² Now the Scripture passage he was reading was this:

> He was led like a sheep to the slaughter,
> and as a lamb is silent before its shearer,
> so He does not open His mouth.
> ³³ In His humiliation justice was denied Him.
> Who will describe His generation?
> For His life is taken from the earth.

³⁴ The eunuch replied to Philip, "I ask you, who is the prophet saying this about—himself or another person?" ³⁵ So Philip proceeded to tell him the good news about Jesus, beginning from that Scripture.

³⁶ As they were traveling down the road, they came to some water. The eunuch said, "Look, there's water! What would keep me from being baptized?" [³⁷ And Philip said, "If you believe with all your heart you may." And he replied, "I believe that Jesus Christ is the Son of God."]* ³⁸ Then he ordered the chariot to stop, and both Philip and the eunuch went down into the water, and he baptized him. ³⁹ When they came up out of the water, the Spirit of the Lord carried Philip away, and the eunuch did not see him any longer. But he went on his way rejoicing. ⁴⁰ Philip appeared in Azotus, and he was traveling and evangelizing all the towns until he came to Caesarea.

## 2 PETER 1:16-21

### THE TRUSTWORTHY PROPHETIC WORD

¹⁶ For we did not follow cleverly contrived myths when we made known to you the power and coming of our Lord Jesus Christ; instead, we were eyewitnesses of His majesty. ¹⁷ For when He received honor and glory from God the Father, a voice came to Him from the Majestic Glory:

> This is My beloved Son.
> I take delight in Him!

¹⁸ And we heard this voice when it came from heaven while we were with Him on the holy mountain. ¹⁹ So we have the prophetic word strongly confirmed. You will do well to pay attention to it, as to a lamp shining in a dismal place, until the day dawns and the morning star rises in your hearts. ²⁰ First of all, you should know this: No prophecy of Scripture comes from one's own interpretation, ²¹ because no prophecy ever came by the will of man; instead, men spoke from God as they were moved by the Holy Spirit.

*Some manuscripts omit bracketed text.*

# 2

## From Dust to Dust

"Remember that you are dust, and to dust you shall return."

These are the words a priest utters as he smears a cross of ashes onto his congregant's forehead during an Ash Wednesday service. It's a somber declaration. In fact, some instead say: "Remember that you have to die."

For more than a thousand years, Christians around the world have begun the Lenten season this way: with the sober acknowledgement that with humanity came sin, and with sin came death. We are free, but not required, to do the same.

**So what is Ash Wednesday, and why do many Christians observe it?**

**Ash Wednesday is a day of repentance.** During Lent, we focus on our need for the death and resurrection of Jesus; we focus on our need to be forgiven. Ash Wednesday is a day where we take a page from the book of Job and repent in dust and ashes (Job 42:6). We remember that from the dust we were made and to the dust we shall return (Genesis 3:19). We remember that we have all sinned and fallen short of God's glory, and yes, we all must die (Romans 3:23).

**Ash Wednesday is a day of hope.** Without Christ, "remember that you have to die" are hard words. But with Christ, they are a reminder that, though our bodies will one day return to dust, we have already been given the hope of the resurrection (1 Corinthians 15:22).

**Ash Wednesday is an opportunity to publicly profess our faith.** The ashen cross the congregant wears is an outward sign of both repentance and hope. People see the mark of the cross at their work, in class, and at the grocery store. Wearing the ashes is a way to repent of our rebellion against God and "confess our sins one to another" (James 5:16).

On Ash Wednesday we admit our limits and acknowledge the brevity of this life. Whether in a formal Ash Wednesday service or privately in our homes, we can use tomorrow, the first day of the Lenten season, to remember that from the dust we were made and to the dust we shall return. Even so, in Christ, we live in the eternal hope of the resurrection. 📖

GENESIS 3:17-19

[17] And He said to Adam, "Because you listened to your wife's voice and ate from the tree about which I commanded you, 'Do not eat from it':

The ground is cursed because of you.
You will eat from it by means of painful labor
all the days of your life.
[18] It will produce thorns and thistles for you,
and you will eat the plants of the field.
[19] You will eat bread by the sweat of your brow
until you return to the ground,
since you were taken from it.
For you are dust,
and you will return to dust."

JOB 42:1-6

JOB REPLIES TO THE LORD

[1] Then Job replied to the Lord:

[2] I know that You can do anything
and no plan of Yours can be thwarted.
[3] You asked, "Who is this who conceals My
counsel with ignorance?"
Surely I spoke about things I did not
understand,
things too wonderful for me to know.
[4] You said, "Listen now, and I will speak.
When I question you, you will inform Me."
[5] I had heard rumors about You,
but now my eyes have seen You.
[6] Therefore I take back my words
and repent in dust and ashes.

ROMANS 3:23

*For all have sinned and fall short of
the glory of God.*

JAMES 5:13-16

EFFECTIVE PRAYER

[13] Is anyone among you suffering? He should pray. Is anyone cheerful? He should sing praises. [14] Is anyone among you sick? He should call for the elders of the church, and they should pray over him after anointing him with olive oil in the name of the Lord. [15] The prayer of faith will save the sick person, and the Lord will restore him to health; if he has committed sins, he will be forgiven. [16] Therefore, confess your sins to one another and pray for one another, so that you may be healed. The urgent request of a righteous person is very powerful in its effect.

NOTES

# 3

## *Judah on Trial*

/ *WEEK ONE*

¹ The vision concerning Judah and Jerusalem that Isaiah son of Amoz saw during the reigns of Uzziah, Jotham, Ahaz, and Hezekiah, kings of Judah.

### JUDAH ON TRIAL

² Listen, heavens, and pay attention, earth,
for the Lord has spoken:
"I have raised children and brought them up,
but they have rebelled against Me.
³ The ox knows its owner,
and the donkey its master's feeding trough,
but Israel does not know;
My people do not understand."

⁴ Oh sinful nation,
people weighed down with iniquity,
brood of evildoers,
depraved children!
They have abandoned the Lord;
they have despised the Holy One of Israel;
they have turned their backs on Him.

⁵ Why do you want more beatings?
Why do you keep on rebelling?
The whole head is hurt,
and the whole heart is sick.
⁶ From the sole of the foot even to the head,
no spot is uninjured—
wounds, welts, and festering sores
not cleansed, bandaged,
or soothed with oil.

⁷ Your land is desolate,
your cities burned with fire;
foreigners devour your fields
before your very eyes—
a desolation demolished by foreigners.
⁸ Daughter Zion is abandoned
like a shelter in a vineyard,
like a shack in a cucumber field,
like a besieged city.

⁹ If the Lord of Hosts
had not left us a few survivors,
we would be like Sodom,
we would resemble Gomorrah.

¹⁰ Hear the word of the Lord,
you rulers of Sodom!
Listen to the instruction of our God,
you people of Gomorrah!
¹¹ "What are all your sacrifices to Me?"
asks the Lord.
"I have had enough of burnt offerings and rams
and the fat of well-fed cattle;
I have no desire for the blood of bulls,
lambs, or male goats.
¹² When you come to appear before Me,
who requires this from you—
this trampling of My courts?
¹³ Stop bringing useless offerings.
Your incense is detestable to Me.
New Moons and Sabbaths,
and the calling of solemn assemblies—
I cannot stand iniquity with a festival.
¹⁴ I hate your New Moons and prescribed festivals.
They have become a burden to Me;
I am tired of putting up with them.
¹⁵ When you lift up your hands in prayer,
I will refuse to look at you;
even if you offer countless prayers,
I will not listen.
Your hands are covered with blood.

seek JUSTICE.

PURIFICATION OF JERUSALEM

¹⁶ "Wash yourselves. Cleanse yourselves.
Remove your evil deeds from My sight.
Stop doing evil.
¹⁷ Learn to do what is good.
Seek justice.
Correct the oppressor.
Defend the rights of the fatherless.
Plead the widow's cause.

¹⁸ "Come, let us discuss this,"
says the Lord.
"Though your sins are like scarlet,
they will be as white as snow;
though they are as red as crimson,
they will be like wool.
¹⁹ If you are willing and obedient,
you will eat the good things of the land.
²⁰ But if you refuse and rebel,
you will be devoured by the sword."
For the mouth of the Lord has spoken.

²¹ The faithful city—
what an adulteress she has become!
She was once full of justice.
Righteousness once dwelt in her—
but now, murderers!
²² Your silver has become dross,
your beer is diluted with water.
²³ Your rulers are rebels,
friends of thieves.
They all love graft
and chase after bribes.
They do not defend the rights of the fatherless,
and the widow's case never comes before them.

²⁴ Therefore the Lord God of Hosts,
the Mighty One of Israel, declares:
"Ah, I will gain satisfaction from My foes;
I will take revenge against My enemies.
²⁵ I will turn My hand against you
and will burn away your dross completely;
I will remove all your impurities.

<sup>26</sup> I will restore your judges to what they once were,
and your advisers to their former state.
Afterward you will be called the Righteous City,
a Faithful City."

<sup>27</sup> Zion will be redeemed by justice,
her repentant ones by righteousness.
<sup>28</sup> But both rebels and sinners will be destroyed,
and those who abandon the Lord will perish.
<sup>29</sup> Indeed, they will be ashamed of the sacred trees
you desired,
and you will be embarrassed because of the gardens
you have chosen.
<sup>30</sup> For you will become like an oak
whose leaves are withered,
and like a garden without water.
<sup>31</sup> The strong one will become tinder,
and his work a spark;
both will burn together,
with no one to quench the flames.

## ISAIAH 2

### THE CITY OF PEACE

<sup>1</sup> The vision that Isaiah son of Amoz saw concerning Judah
and Jerusalem:

<sup>2</sup> In the last days
the mountain of the Lord's house will be established
at the top of the mountains
and will be raised above the hills.
All nations will stream to it,
<sup>3</sup> and many peoples will come and say,
"Come, let us go up to the mountain of the Lord,
to the house of the God of Jacob.
He will teach us about His ways
so that we may walk in His paths."
For instruction will go out of Zion
and the word of the Lord from Jerusalem.
<sup>4</sup> He will settle disputes among the nations
and provide arbitration for many peoples.
They will turn their swords into plows
and their spears into pruning knives.
Nations will not take up the sword against other nations,
and they will never again train for war.

### THE DAY OF THE LORD

<sup>5</sup> House of Jacob,
come and let us walk in the Lord's light.
<sup>6</sup> For You have abandoned Your people,
the house of Jacob,
because they are full of divination from the East
and of fortune-tellers like the Philistines.
They are in league with foreigners.
<sup>7</sup> Their land is full of silver and gold,
and there is no limit to their treasures;
their land is full of horses,
and there is no limit to their chariots.
<sup>8</sup> Their land is full of idols;
they bow down to the work of their hands,
to what their fingers have made.
<sup>9</sup> So humanity is brought low,
and man is humbled.
Do not forgive them!
<sup>10</sup> Go into the rocks
and hide in the dust
from the terror of the Lord
and from His majestic splendor.

<sup>11</sup> *Human pride will be humbled,*
*and the loftiness of men will be brought low;*
*the Lord alone will be exalted on that day.*

<sup>12</sup> For a day belonging to the Lord of Hosts is coming
against all that is proud and lofty,
against all that is lifted up—it will be humbled—
<sup>13</sup> against all the cedars of Lebanon,
lofty and lifted up,
against all the oaks of Bashan,
<sup>14</sup> against all the high mountains,
against all the lofty hills,
<sup>15</sup> against every high tower,
against every fortified wall,
<sup>16</sup> against every ship of Tarshish,
and against every splendid sea vessel.
<sup>17</sup> So human pride will be brought low,
and the loftiness of men will be humbled;
the Lord alone will be exalted on that day.
<sup>18</sup> The idols will vanish completely.

[19] People will go into caves in the rocks

and holes in the ground,

away from the terror of the Lord

and from His majestic splendor,

when He rises to terrify the earth.

[20] On that day people will throw

their silver and gold idols,

which they made to worship,

to the moles and the bats.

[21] They will go into the caves of the rocks

and the crevices in the cliffs,

away from the terror of the Lord

and from His majestic splendor,

when He rises to terrify the earth.

[22] Put no more trust in man,

who has only the breath in his nostrils.

What is he really worth?

## PSALM 68:16-18

[16] Why gaze with envy, you mountain peaks,

at the mountain God desired for His dwelling?

The Lord will live there forever!

[17] God's chariots are tens of thousands,

thousands and thousands;

the Lord is among them in the sanctuary

as He was at Sinai.

[18] You ascended to the heights, taking away captives;

You received gifts from people,

even from the rebellious,

so that the Lord God might live there.

## LUKE 24:44-49

[44] Then He told them, "These are My words that I spoke to you while I was still with you—that everything written about Me in the Law of Moses, the Prophets, and the Psalms must be fulfilled." [45] Then He opened their minds to understand the Scriptures. [46] He also said to them, "This is what is written: The Messiah would suffer and rise from the dead the third day, [47] and repentance for forgiveness of sins would be proclaimed in His name to all the nations, beginning at Jerusalem. [48] You are witnesses of these things. [49] And look, I am sending you what My Father promised. As for you, stay in the city until you are empowered from on high."

## Judah's Leaders Judged

/ WEEK ONE

JUDAH'S LEADERS JUDGED

¹ Observe this: The Lord God of Hosts
is about to remove from Jerusalem and from Judah
every kind of security:
the entire supply of bread and water,
² the hero and warrior,
the judge and prophet,
the fortune-teller and elder,
³ the commander of 50 and the dignitary,
the counselor, cunning magician, and necromancer.

⁴ *"I will make youths their leaders,*
*and the unstable will govern them."*

⁵ The people will oppress one another,
man against man, neighbor against neighbor;
the youth will act arrogantly toward the elder,
and the worthless toward the honorable.
⁶ A man will even seize his brother
in his father's house, saying:
"You have a cloak—you be our leader!
This heap of rubble will be under your control."
⁷ On that day he will cry out, saying:
"I'm not a healer.
I don't even have food or clothing in my house.
Don't make me the leader of the people!"
⁸ For Jerusalem has stumbled
and Judah has fallen
because they have spoken and acted against the Lord,
defying His glorious presence.
⁹ The look on their faces testifies against them,
and like Sodom, they flaunt their sin.
They do not conceal it.
Woe to them,
for they have brought evil on themselves.
¹⁰ Tell the righteous that it will go well for them,
for they will eat the fruit of their labor.
¹¹ Woe to the wicked—it will go badly for them,
for what they have done will be done to them.
¹² Youths oppress My people,
and women rule over them.
My people, your leaders mislead you;
they confuse the direction of your paths.

*Continued*

# MAN OF SORROWS! WHAT A NAME

TEXT AND TUNE: PHILIP BLISS, 1875

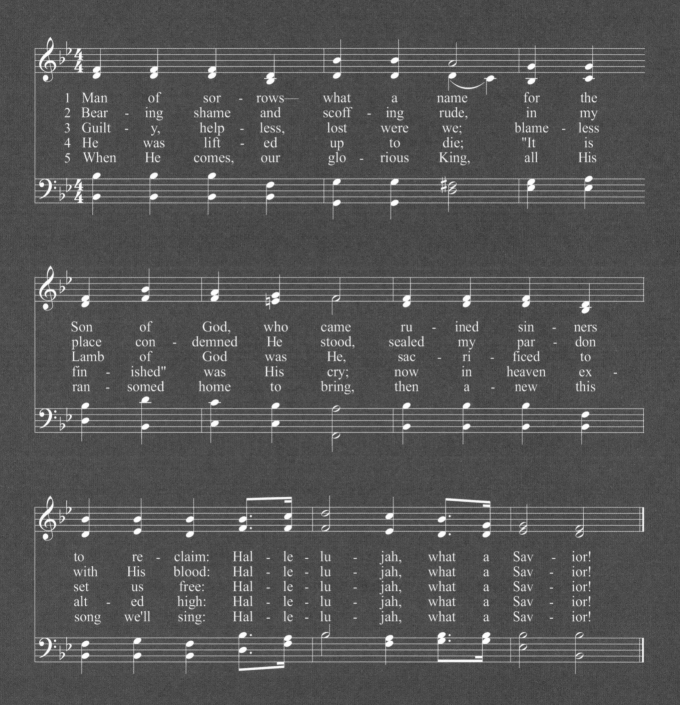

1 Man of sor - rows— what a name for the Son of God, who came ru - ined sin - ners to re - claim: Hal - le - lu - jah, what a Sav - ior!

2 Bear - ing shame and scoff - ing rude, in my place con - demned He stood, sealed my par - don with His blood: Hal - le - lu - jah, what a Sav - ior!

3 Guilt - y, help - less, lost were we; blame - less Lamb of God was He, sac - ri - ficed to set us free: Hal - le - lu - jah, what a Sav - ior!

4 He was lift - ed up to die; "It is fin - ished" was His cry; now in heaven ex - alt - ed high: Hal - le - lu - jah, what a Sav - ior!

5 When He comes, our glo - rious King, all His ran - somed home to bring, then a - new this song we'll sing: Hal - le - lu - jah, what a Sav - ior!

¹³ The Lord rises to argue the case
and stands to judge the people.
¹⁴ The Lord brings this charge
against the elders and leaders of His people:
"You have devastated the vineyard.
The plunder from the poor is in your houses.
¹⁵ Why do you crush My people
and grind the faces of the poor?"

This is the declaration
of the Lord God of Hosts.

### JERUSALEM'S WOMEN JUDGED

¹⁶ The Lord also says:

Because the daughters of Zion are haughty,
walking with heads held high
and seductive eyes,
going along with prancing steps,
jingling their ankle bracelets,
¹⁷ the Lord will put scabs on the heads
of the daughters of Zion,
and the Lord will shave their foreheads bare.

¹⁸ On that day the Lord will strip their finery: ankle bracelets, headbands, crescents, ¹⁹ pendants, bracelets, veils, ²⁰ headdresses, ankle jewelry, sashes, perfume bottles, amulets, ²¹ signet rings, nose rings, ²² festive robes, capes, cloaks, purses, ²³ garments, linen clothes, turbans, and veils.

²⁴ Instead of perfume there will be a stench;
instead of a belt, a rope;
instead of beautifully styled hair, baldness;
instead of fine clothes, sackcloth;
instead of beauty, branding.
²⁵ Your men will fall by the sword,
your warriors in battle.
²⁶ Then her gates will lament and mourn;
deserted, she will sit on the ground.

## ISAIAH 4

¹ On that day seven women
will seize one man, saying,
"We will eat our own bread
and provide our own clothing.
Just let us be called by your name.
Take away our disgrace."

### ZION'S FUTURE GLORY

² On that day the Branch of the Lord will be beautiful and glorious, and the fruit of the land will be the pride and glory of Israel's survivors. ³ Whoever remains in Zion and whoever is left in Jerusalem will be called holy—all in Jerusalem who are destined to live— ⁴ when the Lord has washed away the filth of the daughters of Zion and cleansed the bloodguilt from the heart of Jerusalem by a spirit of judgment and a spirit of burning. ⁵ Then the Lord will create a cloud of smoke by day and a glowing flame of fire by night over the entire site of Mount Zion and over its assemblies. For there will be a canopy over all the glory, ⁶ and there will be a booth for shade from heat by day, and a refuge and shelter from storm and rain.

## EXODUS 13:21-22

²¹ The Lord went ahead of them in a pillar of cloud to lead them on their way during the day and in a pillar of fire to give them light at night, so that they could travel day or night. ²² The pillar of cloud by day and the pillar of fire by night never left its place in front of the people.

## HEBREWS 10:10-14

¹⁰ By this will of God, we have been sanctified through the offering of the body of Jesus Christ once and for all.

¹¹ Every priest stands day after day ministering and offering the same sacrifices time after time, which can never take away sins.

¹² *But this man, after offering one sacrifice for sins forever, sat down at the right hand of God. ¹³ He is now waiting until His enemies are made His footstool. ¹⁴ For by one offering He has perfected forever those who are sanctified.*

NOTES

DATE    /    /

# Isaiah's Call

/ WEEK ONE

ISAIAH 5

SONG OF THE VINEYARD

¹ I will sing about the one I love,
a song about my loved one's vineyard:
The one I love had a vineyard
on a very fertile hill.
² He broke up the soil, cleared it of stones,
and planted it with the finest vines.
He built a tower in the middle of it
and even dug out a winepress there.
He expected it to yield good grapes,
but it yielded worthless grapes.

³ So now, residents of Jerusalem
and men of Judah,
please judge between Me
and My vineyard.
⁴ What more could I have done for My vineyard
than I did?
Why, when I expected a yield of good grapes,
did it yield worthless grapes?
⁵ Now I will tell you
what I am about to do to My vineyard:
I will remove its hedge,
and it will be consumed;
I will tear down its wall,
and it will be trampled.
⁶ I will make it a wasteland.
It will not be pruned or weeded;
thorns and briers will grow up.
I will also give orders to the clouds
that rain should not fall on it.

⁷ *For the vineyard of the Lord of Hosts
is the house of Israel,
and the men of Judah,
the plant He delighted in.
He looked for justice
but saw injustice,
for righteousness,
but heard cries of wretchedness.*

⁸ Woe to those who add house to house
and join field to field
until there is no more room
and you alone are left in the land.

⁹ I heard the Lord of Hosts say:

Indeed, many houses will become desolate,
grand and lovely ones without inhabitants.
¹⁰ For a ten-acre vineyard will yield
only six gallons,
and 10 bushels of seed will yield
only one bushel.

¹¹ Woe to those who rise early in the morning
in pursuit of beer,
who linger into the evening,
inflamed by wine.
¹² At their feasts they have lyre, harp,
tambourine, flute, and wine.
They do not perceive the Lord's actions,
and they do not see the work of His hands.

¹³ Therefore My people will go into exile
because they lack knowledge;
her dignitaries are starving,
and her masses are parched with thirst.
¹⁴ Therefore Sheol enlarges its throat
and opens wide its enormous jaws,
and down go Zion's dignitaries, her masses,
her crowds, and those who carouse in her!
¹⁵ Humanity is brought low, man is humbled,
and haughty eyes are humbled.
¹⁶ But the Lord of Hosts is exalted by His justice,
and the holy God is distinguished by righteousness.
¹⁷ Lambs will graze
as if in their own pastures,
and strangers will eat
among the ruins of the rich.

¹⁸ Woe to those who drag wickedness
with cords of deceit
and pull sin along with cart ropes,
¹⁹ to those who say:

"Let Him hurry up and do His work quickly
so that we can see it!
Let the plan of the Holy One of Israel take place
so that we can know it!"

²⁰ *Woe to those who call evil good*
*and good evil,*
*who substitute darkness for light*
*and light for darkness,*
*who substitute bitter for sweet*
*and sweet for bitter.*

²¹ Woe to those who are wise in their own opinion
and clever in their own sight.
²² Woe to those who are heroes at drinking wine,
who are fearless at mixing beer,
²³ who acquit the guilty for a bribe
and deprive the innocent of justice.

²⁴ Therefore, as a tongue of fire consumes straw
and as dry grass shrivels in the flame,
so their roots will become like something rotten
and their blossoms will blow away like dust,
for they have rejected
the instruction of the Lord of Hosts,
and they have despised
the word of the Holy One of Israel.
²⁵ Therefore the Lord's anger burns against His people.
He raised His hand against them and struck them;
the mountains quaked,
and their corpses were like garbage in the streets.
In all this, His anger is not removed,
and His hand is still raised to strike.

²⁶ He raises a signal flag for the distant nations
and whistles for them from the ends of the earth.
Look—how quickly and swiftly they come!
²⁷ None of them grows weary or stumbles;
no one slumbers or sleeps.
No belt is loose
and no sandal strap broken.
²⁸ Their arrows are sharpened,
and all their bows strung.
Their horses' hooves are like flint;

their chariot wheels are like a whirlwind.
²⁹ Their roaring is like a lion's;
they roar like young lions;
they growl and seize their prey
and carry it off,
and no one can rescue it.
³⁰ On that day they will roar over it,
like the roaring of the sea.
When one looks at the land,
there will be darkness and distress;
light will be obscured by clouds.

## ISAIAH 6

### ISAIAH'S CALL AND MISSION

¹ In the year that King Uzziah died, I saw the Lord seated on a high and lofty throne, and His robe filled the temple. ² Seraphim were standing above Him; each one had six wings: with two he covered his face, with two he covered his feet, and with two he flew. ³ And one called to another:

Holy, holy, holy is the Lord of Hosts;
His glory fills the whole earth.

⁴ The foundations of the doorways shook at the sound of their voices, and the temple was filled with smoke.

⁵ Then I said:

*Woe is me for I am ruined*
*because I am a man of unclean lips*
*and live among a people of unclean lips,*
*and because my eyes have seen the King,*
*the Lord of Hosts.*

⁶ Then one of the seraphim flew to me, and in his hand was a glowing coal that he had taken from the altar with tongs. ⁷ He touched my mouth with it and said:

Now that this has touched your lips,
your wickedness is removed
and your sin is atoned for.

⁸ Then I heard the voice of the Lord saying:

Who should I send?
Who will go for Us?

I said:

Here I am. Send me.

⁹ And He replied:

Go! Say to these people:
Keep listening, but do not understand;
keep looking, but do not perceive.
¹⁰ Dull the minds of these people;
deafen their ears and blind their eyes;
otherwise they might see with their eyes
and hear with their ears,
understand with their minds,
turn back, and be healed.

¹¹ Then I said, "Until when, Lord?" And He replied:

Until cities lie in ruins without inhabitants,
houses are without people,
the land is ruined and desolate,
¹² and the Lord drives the people far away,
leaving great emptiness in the land.
¹³ Though a tenth will remain in the land,
it will be burned again.
Like the terebinth or the oak
that leaves a stump when felled,
the holy seed is the stump.

**PSALM 80:17-19**

¹⁷ Let Your hand be with the man at Your right hand,
with the son of man
You have made strong for Yourself.
¹⁸ Then we will not turn away from You;
revive us, and we will call on Your name.
¹⁹ Restore us, Yahweh, the God of Hosts;
look on us with favor, and we will be saved.

**MATTHEW 21:33-44**

THE PARABLE OF THE VINEYARD OWNER

³³ "Listen to another parable: There was a man, a landowner, who planted a vineyard, put a fence around it, dug a winepress in it, and built a watchtower. He leased it to tenant farmers and went away. ³⁴ When the grape harvest drew near, he sent his slaves to the farmers to collect his fruit. ³⁵ But the farmers took his slaves, beat one, killed another, and stoned a third. ³⁶ Again, he sent other slaves, more than the first group, and they did the same to them. ³⁷ Finally, he sent his son to them. 'They will respect my son,' he said.

³⁸ "But when the tenant farmers saw the son, they said among themselves, 'This is the heir. Come, let's kill him and take his inheritance!' ³⁹ So they seized him, threw him out of the vineyard, and killed him. ⁴⁰ Therefore, when the owner of the vineyard comes, what will he do to those farmers?"

⁴¹ "He will completely destroy those terrible men," they told Him, "and lease his vineyard to other farmers who will give him his produce at the harvest."

⁴² Jesus said to them, "Have you never read in the Scriptures:

The stone that the builders rejected
has become the cornerstone.
This came from the Lord
and is wonderful in our eyes?

⁴³ Therefore I tell you, the kingdom of God will be taken away from you and given to a nation producing its fruit. [⁴⁴ Whoever falls on this stone will be broken to pieces; but on whoever it falls, it will grind him to powder!]"*

* Some manuscripts omit bracketed text.

*DAY* **6**

# GRACE
*day*

Take this day as an opportunity to catch up on your reading, pray, and rest in the presence of the Lord.

*The stone that the builders rejected has become the cornerstone.*

MATTHEW 21:42

SERVES *3*

# PIZZA FRITTATA

## INGREDIENTS:

1 tablespoon butter or ghee
½ cup sliced cremini or button mushrooms
1 cup baby spinach
8 eggs
3 tablespoons almond milk or coconut milk
1 teaspoon parmesan cheese
½ teaspoon dried oregano
¼ teaspoon sea salt
1 tomato, thinly sliced
2 ounces pepperoni

## INSTRUCTIONS:

Preheat oven to 400°F.

Melt the butter in an oven proof 10-inch skillet over medium-high heat. Sauté the mushrooms and spinach for 5 minutes.

Whisk together the eggs, milk, parmesan cheese, oregano, and sea salt, then pour the mixture into the skillet. Remove from the heat and place the tomatoes and pepperoni over top.

Transfer the skillet to the oven and bake for 10 minutes, or until the eggs are cooked through.

*DAY* **7**

# *weekly* TRUTH

Memorizing Scripture is one of the best ways to carry God-breathed truth, instruction, and reproof wherever we go.

In our Lenten study of Isaiah, we are memorizing Scripture about God's calling, judgment, and restoration of His people.

*Then I heard the voice of the Lord saying: Who should I send? Who will go for Us?*

*I said: Here I am. Send me.*

ISAIAH 6:8

*Emily Jeffords, Morning Blooms No. 1, 2015, oil, 4X4, Private Collection*

# 8

## The Lord of Hosts, the Only Refuge

/ WEEK TWO

### THE MESSAGE TO AHAZ

[1] This took place during the reign of Ahaz, son of Jotham, son of Uzziah king of Judah: Rezin king of Aram, along with Pekah, son of Remaliah, king of Israel, waged war against Jerusalem, but he could not succeed. [2] When it became known to the house of David that Aram had occupied Ephraim, the heart of Ahaz and the hearts of his people trembled like trees of a forest shaking in the wind.

[3] Then the Lord said to Isaiah, "Go out with your son Shear-jashub to meet Ahaz at the end of the conduit of the upper pool, by the road to the Fuller's Field. [4] Say to him: Calm down and be quiet. Don't be afraid or cowardly because of these two smoldering stubs of firebrands, the fierce anger of Rezin and Aram, and the son of Remaliah. [5] For Aram, along with Ephraim and the son of Remaliah, has plotted harm against you. They say, [6] 'Let us go up against Judah, terrorize it, and conquer it for ourselves. Then we can install Tabeel's son as king in it.'"

[7] This is what the Lord God says:

> It will not happen; it will not occur.
> [8] The head of Aram is Damascus,
> the head of Damascus is Rezin
> (within 65 years
> Ephraim will be too shattered to be a people),
> [9] the head of Ephraim is Samaria,
> and the head of Samaria is the son of Remaliah.
> If you do not stand firm in your faith,
> then you will not stand at all.

### THE IMMANUEL PROPHECY

[10] Then the Lord spoke again to Ahaz: [11] "Ask for a sign from the Lord your God—from the depths of Sheol to the heights of heaven."

[12] But Ahaz replied, "I will not ask. I will not test the Lord."

[13] Isaiah said, "Listen, house of David! Is it not enough for you to try the patience of men? Will you also try the patience of my God?

*¹⁴ Therefore, the Lord Himself will give you a sign: The virgin will conceive, have a son, and name him Immanuel.*

¹⁵ By the time he learns to reject what is bad and choose what is good, he will be eating butter and honey. ¹⁶ For before the boy knows to reject what is bad and choose what is good, the land of the two kings you dread will be abandoned. ¹⁷ The Lord will bring on you, your people, and the house of your father, such a time as has never been since Ephraim separated from Judah—the king of Assyria is coming."

¹⁸ On that day
the Lord will whistle to the fly
that is at the farthest streams of the Nile
and to the bee that is in the land of Assyria.
¹⁹ All of them will come and settle
in the steep ravines, in the clefts of the rocks,
in all the thornbushes, and in all the water holes.

²⁰ On that day the Lord will use a razor hired from beyond the Euphrates River—the king of Assyria—to shave the head, the hair on the legs, and to remove the beard as well.

²¹ On that day
a man will raise a young cow and two sheep,
²² and from the abundant milk they give
he will eat butter,
for every survivor in the land will eat butter and honey.
²³ And on that day
every place where there were 1,000 vines,
worth 1,000 pieces of silver,
will become thorns and briers.
²⁴ A man will go there with bow and arrows
because the whole land will be thorns and briers.
²⁵ You will not go to all the hills
that were once tilled with a hoe,
for fear of the thorns and briers.
Those hills will be places for oxen to graze
and for sheep to trample.

## ISAIAH 8

### THE COMING ASSYRIAN INVASION

¹ Then the Lord said to me, "Take a large piece of parchment and write on it with an ordinary pen: Maher-shalal-hash-baz. ² I have appointed trustworthy witnesses—Uriah the priest and Zechariah son of Jeberechiah."

³ I was then intimate with the prophetess, and she conceived and gave birth to a son. The Lord said to me, "Name him Maher-shalal-hash-baz, ⁴ for before the boy knows how to call out father or mother, the wealth of Damascus and the spoils of Samaria will be carried off to the king of Assyria."

⁵ The Lord spoke to me again:

⁶ Because these people rejected
the slowly flowing waters of Shiloah
and rejoiced with Rezin
and the son of Remaliah,
⁷ the Lord will certainly bring against them
the mighty rushing waters of the Euphrates River—
the king of Assyria and all his glory.
It will overflow its channels
and spill over all its banks.
⁸ It will pour into Judah,
flood over it, and sweep through,
reaching up to the neck;
and its spreading streams
will fill your entire land, Immanuel!

⁹ Band together, peoples, and be broken;
pay attention, all you distant lands;
prepare for war, and be broken;
prepare for war, and be broken.
¹⁰ Devise a plan; it will fail.
Make a prediction; it will not happen.
For God is with us.

THE LORD OF HOSTS, THE ONLY REFUGE

[11] For this is what the Lord said to me with great power, to keep me from going the way of this people:

[12] Do not call everything an alliance
these people say is an alliance.
Do not fear what they fear;
do not be terrified.
[13] You are to regard only the Lord of Hosts as holy.
Only He should be feared;
only He should be held in awe.
[14] He will be a sanctuary;
but for the two houses of Israel,
He will be a stone to stumble over
and a rock to trip over,
and a trap and a snare to the inhabitants of Jerusalem.
[15] Many will stumble over these;
they will fall and be broken;
they will be snared and captured.

[16] Bind up the testimony.
Seal up the instruction among my disciples.
[17] I will wait for the Lord,
who is hiding His face from the house of Jacob.
I will wait for Him.

[18] Here I am with the children the Lord has given me to be signs and wonders in Israel from the Lord of Hosts who dwells on Mount Zion. [19] When they say to you, "Consult the spirits of the dead and the spiritists who chirp and mutter," shouldn't a people consult their God? Should they consult the dead on behalf of the living? [20] To the law and to the testimony! If they do not speak according to this word, there will be no dawn for them.

[21] They will wander through the land, dejected and hungry. When they are famished, they will become enraged, and, looking upward, will curse their king and their God. [22] They will look toward the earth and see only distress, darkness, and the gloom of affliction, and they will be driven into thick darkness.

**HEBREWS 9:24**

For the Messiah did not enter a sanctuary made with hands (only a model of the true one) but into heaven itself, so that He might now appear in the presence of God for us.

**1 PETER 1:14-16**

[14] As obedient children, do not be conformed to the desires of your former ignorance. [15] But as the One who called you is holy, you also are to be holy in all your conduct; [16] for it is written, Be holy, because I am holy.

name him
IMMANUEL.

NOTES

DATE      /      /

# 9

## *A Great Light*

### BIRTH OF THE PRINCE OF PEACE

<sup>1</sup> Nevertheless, the gloom of the distressed land will not be like that of the former times when He humbled the land of Zebulun and the land of Naphtali. But in the future He will bring honor to the Way of the Sea, to the land east of the Jordan, and to Galilee of the nations.

<sup>2</sup> The people walking in darkness
have seen a great light;
a light has dawned
on those living in the land of darkness.
<sup>3</sup> You have enlarged the nation
and increased its joy.
The people have rejoiced before You
as they rejoice at harvest time
and as they rejoice when dividing spoils.
<sup>4</sup> For You have shattered their oppressive yoke
and the rod on their shoulders,
the staff of their oppressor,
just as You did on the day of Midian.
<sup>5</sup> For the trampling boot of battle
and the bloodied garments of war
will be burned as fuel for the fire.

<sup>6</sup> *For a child will be born for us,*
*a son will be given to us,*
*and the government will be on*
    *His shoulders.*
*He will be named*
*Wonderful Counselor, Mighty God,*
*Eternal Father, Prince of Peace.*

<sup>7</sup> The dominion will be vast,
and its prosperity will never end.
He will reign on the throne of David
and over his kingdom,
to establish and sustain it
with justice and righteousness from now on and forever.
The zeal of the Lord of Hosts will accomplish this.

[8] The Lord sent a message against Jacob;
it came against Israel.
[9] All the people—
Ephraim and the inhabitants of Samaria—will know it.
They will say with pride and arrogance:
[10] "The bricks have fallen,
but we will rebuild with cut stones;
the sycamores have been cut down,
but we will replace them with cedars."
[11] The Lord has raised up Rezin's adversaries against him
and stirred up his enemies.
[12] Aram from the east and Philistia from the west
have consumed Israel with open mouths.
In all this, His anger is not removed,
and His hand is still raised to strike.

[13] The people did not turn to Him who struck them;
they did not seek the Lord of Hosts.
[14] So the Lord cut off Israel's head and tail,
palm branch and reed in a single day.
[15] The head is the elder, the honored one;
the tail is the prophet, the lying teacher.
[16] The leaders of the people mislead them,
and those they mislead are swallowed up.
[17] Therefore the Lord does not rejoice
over Israel's young men
and has no compassion
on its fatherless and widows,
for everyone is a godless evildoer,
and every mouth speaks folly.
In all this, His anger is not removed,
and His hand is still raised to strike.

[18] *For wickedness burns like a fire*
*that consumes thorns and briers*
*and kindles the forest thickets*
*so that they go up in a column of smoke.*

# a LIGHT has dawned

[19] The land is scorched
by the wrath of the Lord of Hosts,
and the people are like fuel for the fire.
No one has compassion on his brother.
[20] They carve meat on the right,
but they are still hungry;
they have eaten on the left,
but they are still not satisfied.
Each one eats the flesh of his own arm.
[21] Manasseh is with Ephraim,
and Ephraim with Manasseh;
together, both are against Judah.
In all this, His anger is not removed,
and His hand is still raised to strike.

## ISAIAH 10:1-4

[1] Woe to those enacting crooked statutes
and writing oppressive laws
[2] to keep the poor from getting a fair trial
and to deprive the afflicted among my people of justice,
so that widows can be their spoil
and they can plunder the fatherless.
[3] What will you do on the day of punishment
when devastation comes from far away?
Who will you run to for help?
Where will you leave your wealth?
[4] There will be nothing to do
except crouch among the prisoners
or fall among the slain.
In all this, His anger is not removed,
and His hand is still raised to strike.

## PSALM 2

CORONATION OF THE SON

[1] Why do the nations rebel
and the peoples plot in vain?
[2] The kings of the earth take their stand,
and the rulers conspire together
against the Lord and His Anointed One:
[3] "Let us tear off their chains
and free ourselves from their restraints."

[4] The One enthroned in heaven laughs;
the Lord ridicules them.
[5] Then He speaks to them in His anger
and terrifies them in His wrath:
[6] "I have consecrated My King
on Zion, My holy mountain."

[7] I will declare the Lord's decree:
He said to Me, "You are My Son;
today I have become Your Father.
[8] Ask of Me,
and I will make the nations Your inheritance
and the ends of the earth Your possession.
[9] You will break them with a rod of iron;
You will shatter them like pottery."

[10] So now, kings, be wise;
receive instruction, you judges of the earth.

*[11] Serve the Lord with reverential awe*
*and rejoice with trembling.*

[12] Pay homage to the Son or He will be angry
and you will perish in your rebellion,
for His anger may ignite at any moment.
All those who take refuge in Him are happy.

## JOHN 3:19-21

[19] This, then, is the judgment: The light has come into the world, and people loved darkness rather than the light because their deeds were evil. [20] For everyone who practices wicked things hates the light and avoids it, so that his deeds may not be exposed. [21] But anyone who lives by the truth comes to the light, so that his works may be shown to be accomplished by God.

# PROPHECIES from Isaiah fulfilled in JESUS

The book of Isaiah is full of promises from God that were fulfilled in the New Testament. Here are just a handful of Isaiah's prophecies fulfilled in the person of Christ.

| PROPHECY | FULFILLMENT |
| --- | --- |
| **BORN OF A VIRGIN** *1* <br><br> Therefore, the Lord Himself will give you a sign: The virgin will conceive, have a son, and name him Immanuel. <br><br> ISAIAH 7:14 | The virgin's name was Mary. And the angel came to her and said, "Rejoice, favored woman! The Lord is with you… You will conceive and give birth to a son, and you will call His name Jesus." <br><br> LUKE 1:27-31 |
| **HARD HEARTS** *2* <br><br> Go! Say to these people: Keep listening, but do not understand; keep looking, but do not perceive. <br><br> ISAIAH 6:9 | For this people's heart has grown callous; their ears are hard of hearing, and they have shut their eyes. <br><br> MATTHEW 13:15 |
| **HEIR TO THE THRONE OF DAVID** *3* <br><br> The dominion will be vast, and its prosperity will never end. He will reign on the throne of David and over his kingdom, to establish and sustain it with justice and righteousness from now on and forever. The zeal of the Lord of Hosts will accomplish this. <br><br> ISAIAH 9:7 | Then the angel told her…"You will conceive and give birth to a son, and you will call His name Jesus. He will be great and will be called the Son of the Most High, and the Lord God will give Him the throne of His father David." <br><br> LUKE 1:30-32 |
| **GOD'S SPIRIT** *4* <br><br> The Spirit of the Lord will rest on Him—a Spirit of wisdom and understanding, a Spirit of counsel and strength, a Spirit of knowledge and of the fear of the Lord. <br><br> ISAIAH 11:2 | As soon as He came up out of the water, He saw the heavens being torn open and the Spirit descending to Him like a dove. <br><br> MARK 1:10 |

NOTES

DATE ___ / ___ / ___

| PROPHECY | FULFILLMENT |
|---|---|

**THE LAME WALK**

*5*

Then the lame will leap like a deer, and the tongue of the mute will sing for joy, for water will gush in the wilderness, and streams in the desert.

ISAIAH 35:6

He told the paralytic, "I tell you: get up, pick up your mat, and go home." Immediately he got up, picked up the mat, and went out in front of everyone. As a result, they were all astounded and gave glory to God, saying, "We have never seen anything like this!"

MARK 2:10-12

---

**THE WAY PREPARED**

*6*

A voice of one crying out: Prepare the way of the Lord in the wilderness; make a straight highway for our God in the desert.

ISAIAH 40:3

"Who are you, then?" they asked. "We need to give an answer to those who sent us. What can you tell us about yourself?"

[John the Baptist] said, "I am a voice of one crying out in the wilderness: Make straight the way of the Lord—just as Isaiah the prophet said."

JOHN 1:22-23

---

**REJECTED**

*7*

He was despised and rejected by men, a man of suffering who knew what sickness was. He was like someone people turned away from; He was despised, and we didn't value Him.

ISAIAH 53:3

He came to His own, and His own people did not receive Him.

JOHN 1:11

---

**CRUCIFIED WITH SINNERS**

*8*

Therefore I will give Him the many as a portion, and He will receive the mighty as spoil, because He submitted Himself to death, and was counted among the rebels; yet He bore the sin of many and interceded for the rebels.

ISAIAH 53:12

They crucified two criminals with Him, one on His right and one on His left. So the Scripture was fulfilled that says: And He was counted among outlaws.

MARK 15:27-28

---

**WOUNDED HEALER**

*9*

But He was pierced because of our transgressions, crushed because of our iniquities; punishment for our peace was on Him, and we are healed by His wounds.

ISAIAH 53:5

He Himself bore our sins in His body on the tree, so that, having died to sins, we might live for righteousness; you have been healed by His wounds.

1 PETER 2:24

---

**SILENT**

*10*

He was oppressed and afflicted, yet He did not open His mouth.

ISAIAH 53:7

But Jesus kept silent.

MATTHEW 26:63

---

# 10

## *The Root of Jesse*

ISAIAH 10:5-34

ASSYRIA, THE INSTRUMENT OF WRATH

⁵ Woe to Assyria, the rod of My anger—
the staff in their hands is My wrath.
⁶ I will send him against a godless nation;
I will command him to go
against a people destined for My rage,
to take spoils, to plunder,
and to trample them down like clay in the streets.
⁷ But this is not what he intends;
this is not what he plans.
It is his intent to destroy
and to cut off many nations.
⁸ For he says,
"Aren't all my commanders kings?
⁹ Isn't Calno like Carchemish?
Isn't Hamath like Arpad?
Isn't Samaria like Damascus?
¹⁰ As my hand seized the idolatrous kingdoms,
whose idols exceeded those of Jerusalem and Samaria,
¹¹ and as I did to Samaria and its idols
will I not also do to Jerusalem and its idols?"

JUDGMENT ON ASSYRIA

¹² But when the Lord finishes all His work against Mount Zion and Jerusalem, He will say, "I will punish the king of Assyria for his arrogant acts and the proud look in his eyes." ¹³ For he said:

I have done this by my own strength
and wisdom, for I am clever.
I abolished the borders of nations
and plundered their treasures;
like a mighty warrior, I subjugated the inhabitants.
¹⁴ My hand has reached out, as if into a nest,
to seize the wealth of the nations.
Like one gathering abandoned eggs,
I gathered the whole earth.
No wing fluttered;
no beak opened or chirped.

*15 Does an ax exalt itself*
*above the one who chops with it?*
*Does a saw magnify itself*
*above the one who saws with it?*

It would be like a staff waving the one who lifts it!
It would be like a rod lifting a man who isn't wood!
16 Therefore the Lord God of Hosts
will inflict an emaciating disease
on the well-fed of Assyria,
and He will kindle a burning fire
under its glory.
17 Israel's Light will become a fire,
and its Holy One, a flame.
In one day it will burn up Assyria's thorns and thistles.
18 He will completely destroy
the glory of its forests and orchards
as a sickness consumes a person.
19 The remaining trees of its forest
will be so few in number
that a child could count them.

### THE REMNANT WILL RETURN

20 On that day the remnant of Israel and the survivors of the house of Jacob will no longer depend on the one who struck them, but they will faithfully depend on the Lord, the Holy One of Israel.

21 The remnant will return, the remnant of Jacob,
to the Mighty God.
22 Israel, even if your people were as numerous
as the sand of the sea,
only a remnant of them will return.
Destruction has been decreed;
justice overflows.
23 For throughout the land
the Lord God of Hosts
is carrying out a destruction that was decreed.

24 Therefore, the Lord God of Hosts says this: "My people who dwell in Zion, do not fear Assyria, though he strikes you with a rod and raises his staff over you as the Egyptians did. 25 In just a little while My wrath will be spent and My anger will turn to their destruction." 26 And the Lord of Hosts will brandish a whip against him as He did when He struck Midian at the rock of Oreb; and He will raise His staff over the sea as He did in Egypt.

### GOD WILL JUDGE ASSYRIA

27 On that day
his burden will fall from your shoulders,
and his yoke from your neck.
The yoke will be broken because of fatness.
28 Assyria has come to Aiath
and has gone through Migron,
storing his equipment at Michmash.
29 They crossed over at the ford, saying,
"We will spend the night at Geba."
The people of Ramah are trembling;
those at Gibeah of Saul have fled.
30 Cry aloud, daughter of Gallim!
Listen, Laishah!
Anathoth is miserable.
31 Madmenah has fled.
The inhabitants of Gebim have sought refuge.
32 Today he will stand at Nob,
shaking his fist at the mountain of Daughter Zion,
the hill of Jerusalem.
33 Look, the Lord God of Hosts
will chop off the branches with terrifying power,
and the tall trees will be cut down,
the high trees felled.
34 He is clearing the thickets of the forest with an ax,
and Lebanon with its majesty will fall.

## ISAIAH 11
### REIGN OF THE DAVIDIC KING

1 Then a shoot will grow from the stump of Jesse,
and a branch from his roots will bear fruit.
2 The Spirit of the Lord will rest on Him—
a Spirit of wisdom and understanding,
a Spirit of counsel and strength,
a Spirit of knowledge and of the fear of the Lord.
3 His delight will be in the fear of the Lord.
He will not judge
by what He sees with His eyes,

He will not execute justice

by what He hears with His ears,

⁴ but He will judge the poor righteously

and execute justice for the oppressed of the land.

He will strike the land

with discipline from His mouth,

and He will kill the wicked

with a command from His lips.

⁵ Righteousness will be a belt around His loins;

faithfulness will be a belt around His waist.

⁶ The wolf will live with the lamb,

and the leopard will lie down with the goat.

The calf, the young lion, and the fatling will

be together,

and a child will lead them.

⁷ The cow and the bear will graze,

their young ones will lie down together,

and the lion will eat straw like the ox.

⁸ An infant will play beside the cobra's pit,

and a toddler will put his hand into a snake's den.

⁹ None will harm or destroy another

on My entire holy mountain,

for the land will be as full

of the knowledge of the Lord

as the sea is filled with water.

### ISRAEL REGATHERED

¹⁰ On that day the root of Jesse

will stand as a banner for the peoples.

The nations will seek Him,

and His resting place will be glorious.

¹¹ On that day the Lord will extend His hand a second time to recover—from Assyria, Egypt, Pathros, Cush, Elam, Shinar, Hamath, and the coasts and islands of the west—the remnant of His people who survive.

¹² He will lift up a banner for the nations

and gather the dispersed of Israel;

He will collect the scattered of Judah

from the four corners of the earth.

¹³ Ephraim's envy will cease;

Judah's harassment will end.

Ephraim will no longer be envious of Judah,

and Judah will not harass Ephraim.

¹⁴ But they will swoop down

on the Philistine flank to the west.

Together they will plunder the people of the east.

They will extend their power over Edom and Moab,

and the Ammonites will be their subjects.

¹⁵ The Lord will divide the Gulf of Suez.

He will wave His hand over the Euphrates

with His mighty wind

and will split it into seven streams,

letting people walk through on foot.

¹⁶ There will be a highway for the remnant of

His people

who will survive from Assyria,

as there was for Israel

when they came up from the land of Egypt.

## ISAIAH 12

### A SONG OF PRAISE

¹ On that day you will say:

"I will praise You, Lord,

although You were angry with me.

Your anger has turned away,

and You have had compassion on me.

² Indeed, God is my salvation;

I will trust Him and not be afraid,

for Yah, the Lord,

is my strength and my song.

He has become my salvation."

³ You will joyfully draw water

from the springs of salvation,

⁴ and on that day you will say:

"Give thanks to Yahweh; proclaim His name!

Celebrate His works among the peoples.

Declare that His name is exalted.

⁵ Sing to Yahweh, for He has done glorious things.

Let this be known throughout the earth.

⁶ Cry out and sing, citizen of Zion,

for the Holy One of Israel is among you

in His greatness."

**ROMANS 8:19-22**

[19] For the creation eagerly waits with anticipation for God's sons to be revealed. [20] For the creation was subjected to futility—not willingly, but because of Him who subjected it—in the hope [21] that the creation itself will also be set free from the bondage of corruption into the glorious freedom of God's children. [22] For we know that the whole creation has been groaning together with labor pains until now.

a shoot will GROW from the stump of JESSE

# Israel's Return

/ WEEK TWO

## ISAIAH 13

### AN ORACLE AGAINST BABYLON

¹ An oracle against Babylon that Isaiah son of Amoz saw:

² Lift up a banner on a barren mountain.
Call out to them.
Wave your hand, and they will go
through the gates of the nobles.
³ I have commanded My chosen ones;
I have also called My warriors,
who exult in My triumph,
to execute My wrath.
⁴ Listen, a tumult on the mountains,
like that of a mighty people!
Listen, an uproar among the kingdoms,
like nations being gathered together!
The Lord of Hosts is mobilizing an army for war.
⁵ They are coming from a far land,
from the distant horizon—
the Lord and the weapons of His wrath—
to destroy the whole country.

⁶ Wail! For the day of the Lord is near.
It will come like destruction from the Almighty.
⁷ Therefore everyone's hands will become weak,
and every man's heart will melt.
⁸ They will be horrified;
pain and agony will seize them;
they will be in anguish like a woman in labor.
They will look at each other,
their faces flushed with fear.

⁹ *Look, the day of the Lord is coming—*

cruel, with rage and burning anger—
to make the earth a desolation
and to destroy the sinners on it.
¹⁰ Indeed, the stars of the sky and its constellations
will not give their light.
The sun will be dark when it rises,
and the moon will not shine.
¹¹ I will bring disaster on the world,
and their own iniquity, on the wicked.

I will put an end to the pride of the arrogant
and humiliate the insolence of tyrants.
¹² I will make man scarcer than gold,
and mankind more rare than the gold of Ophir.
¹³ Therefore I will make the heavens tremble,
and the earth will shake from its foundations
at the wrath of the Lord of Hosts,
on the day of His burning anger.
¹⁴ Like wandering gazelles
and like sheep without a shepherd,
each one will turn to his own people,
each one will flee to his own land.
¹⁵ Whoever is found will be stabbed,
and whoever is caught will die by the sword.
¹⁶ Their children will be smashed to death before
their eyes;
their houses will be looted,
and their wives raped.
¹⁷ Look! I am stirring up the Medes against them,
who cannot be bought off with silver
and who have no desire for gold.
¹⁸ Their bows will cut young men to pieces.
They will have no compassion on little ones;
they will not look with pity on children.

¹⁹ And Babylon, the jewel of the kingdoms,
the glory of the pride of the Chaldeans,
will be like Sodom and Gomorrah
when God overthrew them.
²⁰ It will never be inhabited
or lived in from generation to generation;
a nomad will not pitch his tent there,
and shepherds will not let their flocks rest there.
²¹ But desert creatures will lie down there,
and owls will fill the houses.
Ostriches will dwell there,
and wild goats will leap about.
²² Hyenas will howl in the fortresses,
and jackals, in the luxurious palaces.
Babylon's time is almost up;
her days are almost over.

## ISAIAH 14

### ISRAEL'S RETURN

¹ For the Lord will have compassion on Jacob and will choose Israel again. He will settle them on their own land. The foreigner will join them and be united with the house of Jacob. ² The nations will escort Israel and bring it to its homeland. Then the house of Israel will possess them as male and female slaves in the Lord's land. They will make captives of their captors and will rule over their oppressors.

### DOWNFALL OF THE KING OF BABYLON

³ When the Lord gives you rest from your pain, torment, and the hard labor you were forced to do, ⁴ you will sing this song of contempt about the king of Babylon and say:

How the oppressor has quieted down,
and how the raging has become quiet!
⁵ The Lord has broken the staff of the wicked,
the scepter of the rulers.
⁶ It struck the peoples in anger
with unceasing blows.
It subdued the nations in rage
with relentless persecution.
⁷ All the earth is calm and at rest;
people shout with a ringing cry.
⁸ Even the cypresses and the cedars of Lebanon
rejoice over you:
"Since you have been laid low,
no woodcutter has come against us."

⁹ Sheol below is eager to greet your coming.
He stirs up the spirits of the departed for you—
all the rulers of the earth.
He makes all the kings of the nations
rise from their thrones.
¹⁰ They all respond to you, saying:
"You too have become as weak as we are;
you have become like us!
¹¹ Your splendor has been brought down to Sheol,
along with the music of your harps.
Maggots are spread out under you,
and worms cover you."

¹² Shining morning star,
how you have fallen from the heavens!
You destroyer of nations,
you have been cut down to the ground.
¹³ You said to yourself:
"I will ascend to the heavens;
I will set up my throne
above the stars of God.
I will sit on the mount of the gods' assembly,
in the remotest parts of the North.
¹⁴ I will ascend above the highest clouds;
I will make myself like the Most High."
¹⁵ But you will be brought down to Sheol
into the deepest regions of the Pit.

¹⁶ Those who see you will stare at you;
they will look closely at you:
"Is this the man who caused the earth to tremble,
who shook the kingdoms,
¹⁷ who turned the world into a wilderness,
who destroyed its cities
and would not release the prisoners to return home?"
¹⁸ All the kings of the nations
lie in splendor, each in his own tomb.
¹⁹ But you are thrown out without a grave,
like a worthless branch,
covered by those slain with the sword
and dumped into a rocky pit like a trampled corpse.
²⁰ You will not join them in burial,
because you destroyed your land
and slaughtered your own people.
The offspring of evildoers
will never be remembered.
²¹ Prepare a place of slaughter for his sons,
because of the iniquity of their fathers.
They will never rise up to possess a land
or fill the surface of the earth with cities.

²² "I will rise up against them"—this is the declaration of the Lord of Hosts—"and I will cut off from Babylon her reputation, remnant, offspring, and posterity"—this is the Lord's declaration. ²³ "I will make her a swampland and a region for screech owls, and I will sweep her away with a broom of destruction."

This is the declaration of the Lord of Hosts.

ASSYRIA WILL BE DESTROYED

²⁴ The Lord of Hosts has sworn:

As I have purposed, so it will be;
as I have planned it, so it will happen.
²⁵ I will break Assyria in My land;
I will tread him down on My mountain.
Then his yoke will be taken from them,
and his burden will be removed from their shoulders.
²⁶ This is the plan prepared
for the whole earth,
and this is the hand stretched out
against all the nations.
²⁷ The Lord of Hosts Himself has planned it;
therefore, who can stand in its way?
It is His hand that is outstretched,
so who can turn it back?

AN ORACLE AGAINST PHILISTIA

²⁸ In the year that King Ahaz died, this oracle came:

²⁹ Don't rejoice, all of you in Philistia,
because the rod of the one who struck you is broken.
For a viper will come from the root of a snake,
and from its egg comes a flying serpent.
³⁰ Then the firstborn of the poor will be well fed,
and the impoverished will lie down in safety,
but I will kill your root with hunger,
and your remnant will be slain.

[31] Wail, you gates! Cry out, city!

Tremble with fear, all Philistia!

For a cloud of dust is coming from the north,

and there is no one missing from the invader's ranks.

[32] What answer will be given to the messengers from

that nation?

The Lord has founded Zion,

and His afflicted people find refuge in her.

## PSALM 48:9-14

[9] God, within Your temple,

we contemplate Your faithful love.

[10] Your name, God, like Your praise,

reaches to the ends of the earth;

Your right hand is filled with justice.

[11] Mount Zion is glad.

The towns of Judah rejoice

because of Your judgments.

[12] Go around Zion, encircle it;

count its towers,

[13] note its ramparts; tour its citadels

so that you can tell a future generation:

[14] "This God, our God forever and ever—

He will always lead us."

## REVELATION 12:7-9

### THE DRAGON THROWN OUT OF HEAVEN

[7] Then war broke out in heaven: Michael and his angels fought against the dragon. The dragon and his angels also fought, [8] but he could not prevail, and there was no place for them in heaven any longer. [9] So the great dragon was thrown out—the ancient serpent, who is called the Devil and Satan, the one who deceives the whole world. He was thrown to earth, and his angels with him.

# Destruction and Devastation

AN ORACLE AGAINST MOAB

[1] An oracle against Moab:

Ar in Moab is devastated,
destroyed in a night.
Kir in Moab is devastated,
destroyed in a night.
[2] Dibon went up to its temple
to weep at its high places.
Moab wails on Nebo and at Medeba.
Every head is shaved;
every beard is cut off.

*[3] In its streets they wear sackcloth;*
*on its rooftops and in its public squares*
*   everyone wails,*
*falling down and weeping.*

[4] Heshbon and Elealeh cry out;
their voices are heard as far away as Jahaz.
Therefore the soldiers of Moab cry out,
and they tremble.
[5] My heart cries out over Moab,
whose fugitives flee as far as Zoar,
to Eglath-shelishiyah;
they go up the slope of Luhith weeping;
they raise a cry of destruction
on the road to Horonaim.
[6] The waters of Nimrim are desolate;
the grass is withered, the foliage is gone,
and the vegetation has vanished.
[7] So they carry their wealth and belongings
over the Wadi of the Willows.
[8] For their cry echoes
throughout the territory of Moab.
Their wailing reaches Eglaim;
their wailing reaches Beer-elim.
[9] The waters of Dibon are full of blood,
but I will bring on Dibon even more than this—
a lion for those who escape from Moab,
and for the survivors in the land.

## ISAIAH 16

¹ Send lambs to the ruler of the land,
from Sela in the desert
to the mountain of Daughter Zion.
² Like a bird fleeing,
forced from the nest,
the daughters of Moab
will be at the fords of the Arnon.

³ Give us counsel and make a decision.
Shelter us at noonday
with shade that is as dark as night.
Hide the refugees;
do not betray the one who flees.
⁴ Let my refugees stay with you;
be a refuge for Moab from the aggressor.

When the oppressor has gone,
destruction has ended,
and marauders have vanished from the land.
⁵ Then in the tent of David
a throne will be established by faithful love.
A judge who seeks what is right
and is quick to execute justice
will sit on the throne forever.

⁶ We have heard of Moab's pride—
how very proud he is—
his haughtiness, his pride, his arrogance,
and his empty boasting.
⁷ Therefore let Moab wail;
let every one of them wail for Moab.
Mourn, you who are completely devastated,
for the raisin cakes of Kir-hareseth.

⁸ For Heshbon's terraced vineyards
and the grapevines of Sibmah have withered.
The rulers of the nations
have trampled its choice vines
that reached as far as Jazer
and spread to the desert.
Their shoots spread out
and reached the Dead Sea.
⁹ So I join with Jazer
to weep for the vines of Sibmah;
I drench Heshbon and Elealeh with my tears.
Triumphant shouts have fallen silent
over your summer fruit and your harvest.
¹⁰ Joy and rejoicing have been removed from the orchard;
no one is singing or shouting for joy in the vineyards.
No one tramples grapes in the winepresses.
I have put an end to the shouting.
¹¹ Therefore I moan like the sound of a lyre for Moab,
as does my innermost being for Kir-heres.
¹² When Moab appears on the high place,
when he tires himself out
and comes to his sanctuary to pray,
it will do him no good.

¹³ This is the message that the Lord previously announced about Moab. ¹⁴ And now the Lord says, "In three years, as a hired worker counts years, Moab's splendor will become an object of contempt, in spite of a very large population. And those who are left will be few and weak."

## ISAIAH 17

AN ORACLE AGAINST DAMASCUS

¹ An oracle against Damascus:

Look, Damascus is no longer a city.
It has become a ruined heap.
² The cities of Aroer are forsaken;
they will be places for flocks.
They will lie down without fear.
³ The fortress disappears from Ephraim,
and a kingdom from Damascus.

established
by faithful
LOVE.

The remnant of Aram will be
like the splendor of the Israelites.

This is the declaration
of the Lord of Hosts.

### JUDGMENT AGAINST ISRAEL

⁴ On that day
the splendor of Jacob will fade,
and his healthy body will become emaciated.
⁵ It will be as if a reaper had gathered standing grain—
his arm harvesting the heads of grain—
and as if one had gleaned heads of grain
in the Valley of Rephaim.
⁶ Only gleanings will be left in Israel,
as if an olive tree had been beaten—
two or three berries at the very top of the tree,
four or five on its fruitful branches.

This is the declaration of the Lord,
the God of Israel.

⁷ On that day people will look to their Maker and will turn their eyes to the Holy One of Israel. ⁸ They will not look to the altars they made with their hands or to the Asherahs and incense altars they made with their fingers.

⁹ On that day their strong cities will be
like the abandoned woods and mountaintops
that were abandoned because of the Israelites;
there will be desolation.
¹⁰ For you have forgotten the God of your salvation,
and you have failed to remember
the rock of your strength;
therefore you will plant beautiful plants
and set out cuttings from exotic vines.
¹¹ On the day that you plant,
you will help them to grow,
and in the morning
you will help your seed to sprout,
but the harvest will vanish
on the day of disease and incurable pain.

### JUDGMENT AGAINST THE NATIONS

¹² Ah! The roar of many peoples—
they roar like the roaring of the seas.
The raging of the nations—
they rage like the raging of mighty waters.
¹³ The nations rage like the raging of many waters.
He rebukes them, and they flee far away,
driven before the wind like chaff on the hills
and like tumbleweeds before a gale.
¹⁴ In the evening—sudden terror!
Before morning—it is gone!
This is the fate of those who plunder us
and the lot of those who ravage us.

## PSALM 68:19

May the Lord be praised!
Day after day He bears our burdens;
God is our salvation.    *Selah*

## LUKE 21:25-28

### THE COMING OF THE SON OF MAN

²⁵ Then there will be signs in the sun, moon, and stars; and there will be anguish on the earth among nations bewildered by the roaring sea and waves. ²⁶ People will faint from fear and expectation of the things that are coming on the world, because the celestial powers will be shaken. ²⁷ Then they will see the Son of Man coming in a cloud with power and great glory. ²⁸ But when these things begin to take place, stand up and lift up your heads, because your redemption is near!

people will LOOK to their MAKER

NOTES

DATE      /      /

DAY *13*

# GRACE
# *day*

Take this day as an opportunity to catch up on your reading, pray, and rest in the presence of the Lord.

*May the Lord be praised!*
*Day after day He*
*bears our burdens;*
*God is our salvation.* *Selah*

PSALM 68:19

SERVES *4*

# ASPARAGUS BENEDICT

### INGREDIENTS:

8 large asparagus stalks, about 12 ounces
4 large eggs
2 teaspoons apple cider vinegar
chives for garnishing
Hollandaise Sauce*

### INSTRUCTIONS:

Break each egg into a separate small bowl.

Trim the bottom ½-inch of the asparagus stalks, then slice them thinly lengthwise.

Bring a deep skillet of water to a boil. Cook the asparagus in the boiling water for 5 minutes, until bright green and tender.

Remove with a slotted spoon, then add the apple cider vinegar and reduce the heat to a low simmer.

Carefully slide in each egg, one at a time.

Cover the pan, remove from the heat, and allow the eggs to cook for 7-9 minutes, until the whites are set and the yolks are still soft. Drain on a paper towel.

Serve each egg over a plate of asparagus stalks and top with hollandaise and chives.

### *HOLLANDAISE SAUCE

2 large egg yolks
¼ cup melted grassfed butter
2 teaspoons fresh lemon juice
¼ teaspoon paprika
¼ teaspoon sea salt

Pour boiling water into a blender, then cover and let sit for 10 minutes. Dump out the water and dry the container thoroughly.

Blend the egg yolks with the lemon juice, salt, and paprika.

With the blender running on low, slowly pour in the hot melted butter.

Blend for about 30 seconds until the sauce has thickened and the butter is well incorporated. An immersion blender works really well for this as well. The sauce will continue to thicken as it cools.

*DAY* *14*

# *weekly* TRUTH

Memorizing Scripture is one of the best ways to carry God-breathed truth, instruction, and reproof wherever we go.

In our Lenten study of Isaiah, we are memorizing Scripture about God's calling, judgment, and restoration of His people.

*Yahweh, You are my God;*
*I will exalt You.*
*I will praise Your name,*
*for You have accomplished wonders,*
*plans formed long ago,*
*with perfect faithfulness.*
ISAIAH 25:1

*Emily Jeffords, Hope Rising, 2015, oil, 36x48, Private Collection*

# 15

## The Lord Will Make Himself Known

[1] Ah! The land of buzzing insect wings
beyond the rivers of Cush
[2] sends couriers by sea,
in reed vessels on the waters.

Go, swift messengers,
to a nation tall and smooth-skinned,
to a people feared far and near,
a powerful nation with a strange language,
whose land is divided by rivers.
[3] All you inhabitants of the world
and you who live on the earth,
when a banner is raised on the mountains, look!
When a trumpet sounds, listen!

[4] For, the Lord said to me:

*I will quietly look out from My place,*
*like shimmering heat in sunshine,*
*like a rain cloud in harvest heat.*

[5] For before the harvest, when the blossoming is over
and the blossom becomes a ripening grape,
He will cut off the shoots with a pruning knife,
and tear away and remove the branches.
[6] They will all be left for the birds of prey on the hills
and for the wild animals of the land.
The birds will spend the summer on them,
and all the animals, the winter on them.

[7] At that time a gift will be brought to Yahweh of Hosts
from a people tall and smooth-skinned, a people feared
far and near, a powerful nation with a strange language,
whose land is divided by rivers—to Mount Zion, the place
of the name of Yahweh of Hosts.

## ISAIAH 19

### AN ORACLE AGAINST EGYPT

¹ An oracle against Egypt:

Look, the Lord rides on a swift cloud
and is coming to Egypt.
Egypt's idols will tremble before Him,
and Egypt's heart will melt within it.
² I will provoke Egypt against Egypt;
each will fight against his brother
and each against his friend,
city against city, kingdom against kingdom.
³ Egypt's spirit will be disturbed within it,
and I will frustrate its plans.
Then they will seek idols, ghosts,
spirits of the dead, and spiritists.
⁴ I will deliver Egypt into the hands of harsh masters,
and a strong king will rule it.
This is the declaration of the Lord God of Hosts.

⁵ The waters of the sea will dry up,
and the river will be parched and dry.
⁶ The channels will stink;
they will dwindle, and Egypt's canals will be parched.
Reed and rush will die.
⁷ The reeds by the Nile, by the mouth of the river,
and all the cultivated areas of the Nile
will wither, blow away, and vanish.
⁸ Then the fishermen will mourn.
All those who cast hooks into the Nile will lament,
and those who spread nets on the water will shrivel up.
⁹ Those who work with flax will be dismayed;
the combers and weavers will turn pale.
¹⁰ Egypt's weavers will be dejected;
all her wage earners will be demoralized.

¹¹ The princes of Zoan are complete fools;
Pharaoh's wisest advisers give stupid advice!
How can you say to Pharaoh,
"I am one of the wise,
a student of eastern kings"?
¹² Where then are your wise men?
Let them tell you and reveal
what the Lord of Hosts has planned against Egypt.

¹³ The princes of Zoan have been fools;
the princes of Memphis are deceived.
Her tribal chieftains have led Egypt astray.
¹⁴ The Lord has mixed within her a spirit of confusion.
The leaders have made Egypt stagger in all she does,
as a drunkard staggers in his vomit.
¹⁵ No head or tail, palm or reed,
will be able to do anything for Egypt.

### EGYPT WILL KNOW THE LORD

¹⁶ On that day Egypt will be like women. She will tremble with fear because of the threatening hand of the Lord of Hosts when He raises it against her. ¹⁷ The land of Judah will terrify Egypt; whenever Judah is mentioned, Egypt will tremble because of what the Lord of Hosts has planned against it.

¹⁸ On that day five cities in the land of Egypt will speak the language of Canaan and swear loyalty to the Lord of Hosts. One of the cities will be called the City of the Sun.

¹⁹ On that day there will be an altar to the Lord in the center of the land of Egypt and a pillar to the Lord near her border. ²⁰ It will be a sign and witness to the Lord of Hosts in the land of Egypt. When they cry out to the Lord because of their oppressors, He will send them a savior and leader, and he will rescue them. ²¹ The Lord will make Himself known to Egypt, and Egypt will know the Lord on that day. They will offer sacrifices and offerings; they will make vows to the Lord and fulfill them. ²² The Lord will

strike Egypt, striking and healing. Then they will return to the Lord and He will hear their prayers and heal them.

²³ On that day there will be a highway from Egypt to Assyria. Assyria will go to Egypt, Egypt to Assyria, and Egypt will worship with Assyria.

²⁴ On that day Israel will form a triple alliance with Egypt and Assyria—a blessing within the land. ²⁵ The Lord of Hosts will bless them, saying, "Egypt My people, Assyria My handiwork, and Israel My inheritance are blessed."

## ISAIAH 20

### NO HELP FROM CUSH OR EGYPT

¹ In the year that the chief commander, sent by Sargon king of Assyria, came to Ashdod and attacked and captured it— ² during that time the Lord had spoken through Isaiah son of Amoz, saying, "Go, take off your sackcloth and remove the sandals from your feet," and he did so, going naked and barefoot— ³ the Lord said, "As My servant Isaiah has gone naked and barefoot three years as a sign and omen against Egypt and Cush, ⁴ so the king of Assyria will lead the captives of Egypt and the exiles of Cush, young and old alike, naked and barefoot, with bared buttocks—to Egypt's shame. ⁵ Those who made Cush their hope and Egypt their boast will be dismayed and ashamed. ⁶ And the inhabitants of this coastland will say on that day, 'Look, this is what has happened to those we relied on and fled to for help to rescue us from the king of Assyria! Now, how will we escape?'"

## MATTHEW 10:16-23

### PERSECUTIONS PREDICTED

¹⁶ "Look, I'm sending you out like sheep among wolves. Therefore be as shrewd as serpents and as harmless as doves. ¹⁷ Because people will hand you over to sanhedrins and flog you in their synagogues, beware of them. ¹⁸ You will even be brought before governors and kings because of Me, to bear witness to them and to the nations. ¹⁹ But when they hand you over, don't worry about how or what you should speak. For you will be given what to say at that hour, ²⁰ because you are not speaking, but the Spirit of your Father is speaking through you.

²¹ "Brother will betray brother to death, and a father his child. Children will even rise up against their parents and have them put to death. ²² You will be hated by everyone because of My name. But the one who endures to the end will be delivered. ²³ When they persecute you in one town, escape to another. For I assure you: You will not have covered the towns of Israel before the Son of Man comes."

## ROMANS 9:14-18

### GOD'S SELECTION IS JUST

¹⁴ What should we say then? Is there injustice with God? Absolutely not! ¹⁵ For He tells Moses:

*I will show mercy*
*to whom I will show mercy,*
*and I will have compassion*
*on whom I will have compassion.*

¹⁶ So then it does not depend on human will or effort but on God who shows mercy. ¹⁷ For the Scripture tells Pharaoh:

I raised you up for this reason
so that I may display My power in you
and that My name may be proclaimed in all the earth.

¹⁸ So then, He shows mercy to those He wants to, and He hardens those He wants to harden.

NOTES

DATE     /     /
_____

# 16

## *Judgment Against the Nations*

A JUDGMENT ON BABYLON

[1] An oracle against the desert by the sea:

Like storms that pass over the Negev,
it comes from the desert, from the land of terror.
[2] A troubling vision is declared to me:
"The treacherous one acts treacherously,
and the destroyer destroys.
Advance, Elam! Lay siege, you Medes!
I will put an end to all her groaning."

[3] Therefore I am filled with anguish.
Pain grips me, like the pain of a woman in labor.

*I am too perplexed to hear,*
*too dismayed to see.*

[4] My heart staggers;
horror terrifies me.
He has turned my last glimmer of hope
into sheer terror.
[5] Prepare a table, and spread out a carpet!
Eat and drink!
Rise up, you princes, and oil the shields!

[6] For the Lord has said to me,
"Go, post a lookout;
let him report what he sees.
[7] When he sees riders—
pairs of horsemen,
riders on donkeys,
riders on camels—
he must pay close attention."
[8] Then the lookout reported,
"Lord, I stand on the watchtower all day,
and I stay at my post all night.
[9] Look, riders come—
horsemen in pairs."
And he answered, saying,
"Babylon has fallen, has fallen.
All the images of her gods
have been shattered on the ground."

# Let ME weep BITTERLY!

¹⁰ My people who have been crushed
on the threshing floor,
I have declared to you
what I have heard from the Lord of Hosts,
the God of Israel.

## AN ORACLE AGAINST DUMAH

¹¹ An oracle against Dumah:

One calls to me from Seir,
"Watchman, what is left of the night?
Watchman, what is left of the night?"
¹² The watchman said,
"Morning has come, and also night.
If you want to ask, ask!
Come back again."

## AN ORACLE AGAINST ARABIA

¹³ An oracle against Arabia:

In the desert brush
you will camp for the night,
you caravans of Dedanites.
¹⁴ Bring water for the thirsty.
The inhabitants of the land of Tema
meet the refugees with food.
¹⁵ For they have fled from swords,
from the drawn sword,
from the bow that is strung,
and from the stress of battle.

¹⁶ For the Lord said this to me: "Within one year, as a hired worker counts years, all the glory of Kedar will be gone. ¹⁷ The remaining Kedarite archers will be few in number." For the Lord, the God of Israel, has spoken.

## ISAIAH 22

### AN ORACLE AGAINST JERUSALEM

¹ An oracle against the Valley of Vision:

What's the matter with you?
Why have all of you gone up to the rooftops?
² The noisy city, the jubilant town,
is filled with revelry.
Your dead did not die by the sword;
they were not killed in battle.
³ All your rulers have fled together,
captured without a bow.
All your fugitives were captured together;
they had fled far away.
⁴ Therefore I said,
"Look away from me! Let me weep bitterly!
Do not try to comfort me
about the destruction of my dear people."
⁵ For the Lord God of Hosts
had a day of tumult, trampling, and confusion
in the Valley of Vision—
people shouting and crying to the mountains;
⁶ Elam took up a quiver
with chariots and horsemen,
and Kir uncovered the shield.
⁷ Your best valleys were full of chariots,
and horsemen were positioned at the gates.
⁸ He removed the defenses of Judah.

On that day you looked to the weapons in the House of the Forest. ⁹ You saw that there were many breaches in the walls of the city of David. You collected water from the lower pool. ¹⁰ You counted the houses of Jerusalem so that you could tear them down to fortify the wall. ¹¹ You made a reservoir between the walls for the waters of the ancient pool, but you did not look to the One who made it, or consider the One who created it long ago.

¹² *On that day the Lord God of Hosts called for weeping, for wailing, for shaven heads, and for the wearing of sackcloth.*

[13] But look: joy and gladness,
butchering of cattle, slaughtering of sheep,
eating of meat, and drinking of wine—
"Let us eat and drink, for tomorrow we die!"
[14] The Lord of Hosts has directly revealed to me:
"This sin of yours will never be wiped out."
The Lord God of Hosts has spoken.

### AN ORACLE AGAINST SHEBNA

[15] The Lord God of Hosts said: "Go to Shebna, that steward who is in charge of the palace, and say to him: [16] What are you doing here? Who authorized you to carve out a tomb for yourself here, carving your tomb on the height and cutting a crypt for yourself out of rock? [17] Look, you strong man! The Lord is about to shake you violently. He will take hold of you, [18] wind you up into a ball, and sling you into a wide land. There you will die, and there your glorious chariots will be—a disgrace to the house of your lord. [19] I will remove you from your office; you will be ousted from your position.

[20] "On that day I will call for my servant, Eliakim son of Hilkiah. [21] I will clothe him with your robe and tie your sash around him. I will put your authority into his hand, and he will be like a father to the inhabitants of Jerusalem and to the House of Judah. [22] I will place the key of the House of David on his shoulder; what he opens, no one can close; what he closes, no one can open. [23] I will drive him, like a peg, into a firm place. He will be a throne of honor for his father's house. [24] They will hang on him the whole burden of his father's house: the descendants and the offshoots—all the small vessels, from bowls to every kind of jar. [25] On that day"—the declaration of the Lord of Hosts—"the peg that was driven into a firm place will give way, be cut off, and fall, and the load on it will be destroyed." Indeed, the Lord has spoken.

### 1 CORINTHIANS 15:54

When this corruptible is clothed
with incorruptibility,
and this mortal is clothed
with immortality,
then the saying that is written will take place:
Death has been swallowed up in victory.

### 1 PETER 2:6

For it is contained in Scripture:

Look! I lay a stone in Zion,
a chosen and honored cornerstone,
and the one who believes in Him
will never be put to shame!

NOTES

DATE   /   /

# 17

## The Lord Will Reign as King

AN ORACLE AGAINST TYRE

¹ An oracle against Tyre:

Wail, ships of Tarshish,
for your haven has been destroyed.
Word has reached them from the land of Cyprus.
² Mourn, inhabitants of the coastland,
you merchants of Sidon;
your agents have crossed the sea
³ on many waters.
Tyre's revenue was the grain from Shihor—
the harvest of the Nile.
She was the merchant among the nations.
⁴ Be ashamed Sidon, the stronghold of the sea,
for the sea has spoken:
"I have not been in labor or given birth.
I have not raised young men
or brought up young women."
⁵ When the news reaches Egypt,
they will be in anguish over the news about Tyre.
⁶ Cross over to Tarshish;
wail, inhabitants of the coastland!
⁷ Is this your jubilant city,
whose origin was in ancient times,
whose feet have taken her
to settle far away?
⁸ Who planned this against Tyre,
the bestower of crowns,
whose traders are princes,
whose merchants are the honored ones of the earth?
⁹ The Lord of Hosts planned it,
to desecrate all its glorious beauty,
to disgrace all the honored ones of the earth.
¹⁰ Overflow your land like the Nile, daughter
of Tarshish;
there is no longer anything to restrain you.

¹¹ *He stretched out His hand over the sea;*
*He made kingdoms tremble.*

The Lord has commanded
that the Canaanite fortresses be destroyed.

¹² He said,

"You will not rejoice anymore,

ravished young woman, daughter of Sidon.

Get up and cross over to Cyprus—

even there you will have no rest!"

¹³ Look at the land of the Chaldeans—

a people who no longer exist.

Assyria destined it for desert creatures.

They set up their siege towers

and stripped its palaces.

They made it a ruin.

¹⁴ Wail, ships of Tarshish,

because your fortress is destroyed!

¹⁵ On that day Tyre will be forgotten for 70 years—the life span of one king. At the end of 70 years, what the song says about the prostitute will happen to Tyre:

¹⁶ Pick up your lyre,

stroll through the city,

prostitute forgotten by men.

Play skillfully,

sing many a song,

and you will be thought of again.

¹⁷ And at the end of the 70 years, the Lord will restore Tyre and she will go back into business, prostituting herself with all the kingdoms of the world on the face of the earth. ¹⁸ But her profits and wages will be dedicated to the Lord. They will not be stored or saved, for her profit will go to those who live in the Lord's presence, to provide them with ample food and sacred clothing.

## ISAIAH 24

THE EARTH JUDGED

¹ Look, the Lord is stripping the earth bare

and making it desolate.

He will twist its surface and scatter its inhabitants:

² people and priest alike,

servant and master,

female servant and mistress,

buyer and seller,

lender and borrower,

creditor and debtor.

³ The earth will be stripped completely bare

and will be totally plundered,

for the Lord has spoken this message.

⁴ The earth mourns and withers;

the world wastes away and withers;

the exalted people of the earth waste away.

⁵ The earth is polluted by its inhabitants,

for they have transgressed teachings,

overstepped decrees,

and broken the everlasting covenant.

⁶ Therefore a curse has consumed the earth,

and its inhabitants have become guilty;

the earth's inhabitants have been burned,

and only a few survive.

⁷ The new wine mourns;

the vine withers.

All the carousers now groan.

⁸ The joyful tambourines have ceased.

The noise of the jubilant has stopped.

The joyful lyre has ceased.

⁹ They no longer sing and drink wine;

beer is bitter to those who drink it.

¹⁰ The city of chaos is shattered;

every house is closed to entry.

¹¹ In the streets they cry for wine.

All joy grows dark;

earth's rejoicing goes into exile.

¹² Only desolation remains in the city;

its gate has collapsed in ruins.

¹³ For this is how it will be on earth

among the nations:

like a harvested olive tree,

like a gleaning after a grape harvest.

¹⁴ They raise their voices, they sing out;

they proclaim in the west

the majesty of the Lord.

¹⁵ Therefore, in the east honor the Lord!

In the islands of the west

honor the name of Yahweh,

the God of Israel.

¹⁶ From the ends of the earth we hear songs:

The Splendor of the Righteous One.

# they SING out

But I said, "I waste away! I waste away!
Woe is me."
The treacherous act treacherously;
the treacherous deal very treacherously.

17 Panic, pit, and trap await you
who dwell on the earth.
18 Whoever flees at the sound of panic
will fall into a pit,
and whoever escapes from the pit
will be caught in a trap.
For the windows are opened from heaven,
and the foundations of the earth are shaken.
19 The earth is completely devastated;
the earth is split open;
the earth is violently shaken.
20 The earth staggers like a drunkard
and sways like a hut.
Earth's rebellion weighs it down,
and it falls, never to rise again.

21 On that day the Lord will punish
the host of heaven above
and kings of the earth below.
22 They will be gathered together
like prisoners in a pit.
They will be confined to a dungeon;
after many days they will be punished.
23 The moon will be put to shame
and the sun disgraced,
because the Lord of Hosts will reign as king
on Mount Zion in Jerusalem,
and He will display His glory
in the presence of His elders.

## ROMANS 1:18-23

### THE GUILT OF THE GENTILE WORLD

18 For God's wrath is revealed from heaven against all godlessness and unrighteousness of people who by their unrighteousness suppress the truth, 19 since what can be known about God is evident among them, because God has shown it to them. 20 For His invisible attributes, that is, His eternal power and divine nature, have been clearly seen since the creation of the world, being understood through what He has made. As a result, people are without excuse. 21 For though they knew God, they did not glorify Him as God or show gratitude. Instead, their thinking became nonsense, and their senseless minds were darkened. 22 Claiming to be wise, they became fools 23 and exchanged the glory of the immortal God for images resembling mortal man, birds, four-footed animals, and reptiles.

## PHILIPPIANS 2:5-11

### CHRIST'S HUMILITY AND EXALTATION

5 Make your own attitude that of Christ Jesus,

6 who, existing in the form of God,
did not consider equality with God
as something to be used for His own advantage.
7 Instead He emptied Himself
by assuming the form of a slave,
taking on the likeness of men.
And when He had come as a man
in His external form,
8 He humbled Himself by becoming obedient
to the point of death—
even to death on a cross.
9 For this reason God highly exalted Him
and gave Him the name
that is above every name,
10 so that at the name of Jesus
every knee will bow—
of those who are in heaven and on earth
and under the earth—
11 and every tongue should confess
that Jesus Christ is Lord,
to the glory of God the Father.

NOTES

DATE    /    /

# 18

## Salvation and Judgment

[1] Yahweh, You are my God;
I will exalt You. I will praise Your name,
for You have accomplished wonders,
plans formed long ago, with perfect faithfulness.
[2] For You have turned the city into a pile of rocks,
a fortified city, into ruins;
the fortress of barbarians is no longer a city;
it will never be rebuilt.
[3] Therefore, a strong people will honor You.
The cities of violent nations will fear You.
[4] For You have been a stronghold for the poor,
a stronghold for the needy person in his distress,
a refuge from the rain, a shade from the heat.
When the breath of the violent
is like rain against a wall,
[5] like heat in a dry land,
You subdue the uproar of barbarians.
As the shade of a cloud cools the heat of the day,
so He silences the song of the violent.

[6] The Lord of Hosts will prepare a feast
for all the peoples on this mountain—
a feast of aged wine, choice meat, finely aged wine.
[7] On this mountain
He will destroy the burial shroud,
the shroud over all the peoples,
the sheet covering all the nations;
[8] He will destroy death forever.
The Lord God will wipe away the tears
from every face
and remove His people's disgrace
from the whole earth,
for the Lord has spoken.

[9] On that day it will be said,
"Look, this is our God;
we have waited for Him, and He has saved us.
This is the Lord; we have waited for Him.
Let us rejoice and be glad in His salvation."

[10] For the Lord's power will rest on this mountain.
But Moab will be trampled in his place
as straw is trampled in a dung pile.
[11] He will spread out his arms in the middle of it,
as a swimmer spreads out his arms to swim.
His pride will be brought low,
along with the trickery of his hands.
[12] The high-walled fortress will be brought down,
thrown to the ground, to the dust.

### GENESIS 3:17-19

[17] And He said to Adam, "Because you listened to your wife's voice and ate from the tree about which I commanded you, 'Do not eat from it':

The ground is cursed because of you.
You will eat from it by means of painful labor
all the days of your life.
[18] It will produce thorns and thistles for you,
and you will eat the plants of the field.
[19] You will eat bread by the sweat of your brow
until you return to the ground,
since you were taken from it.
For you are dust,
and you will return to dust."

### HEBREWS 12:22-24

[22] Instead, you have come to Mount Zion, to the city of the living God (the heavenly Jerusalem), to myriads of angels in festive gathering, [23] to the assembly of the firstborn whose names have been written in heaven, to God who is the Judge of all, to the spirits of righteous people made perfect, [24] to Jesus (mediator of a new covenant), and to the sprinkled blood, which says better things than the blood of Abel.

REJOICE and be glad

# O SACRED HEAD, NOW WOUNDED

TEXT: MEDIEVAL    TUNE: JOHANN BACH, 1729

1 O sa-cred head, now wound-ed, with grief and shame weighed down,
2 My Lord, what You did suf-fer was all for sin-ners' gain;
3 What lan-guage shall I bor-row to thank You, dear-est Friend,

now scorn-ful-ly sur-round-ed with thorns, Your on-ly crown.
mine, mine was the trans-gres-sion, but Yours the dead-ly pain.
for this, Your dy-ing sor-row, Your mer-cy with-out end?

O sa-cred head, what glo-ry and bless-ing You have known!
So here I kneel, my Sav-ior, for I de-serve Your place;
Lord, make me Yours for-ev-er, a loy-al ser-vant true,

Yet, though de-spised and gor-y, I claim You as my own.
look on me with Your fa-vor and save me by Your grace.
and let me nev-er, nev-er out-live my love for You.

NOTES

DATE      /      /

# 19

## The Song of Judah

### THE SONG OF JUDAH

¹ On that day this song will be sung in the land of Judah:

> We have a strong city.
> Salvation is established as walls and ramparts.
> ² Open the gates
> so a righteous nation can come in—
> one that remains faithful.
> ³ You will keep the mind that is dependent on You
> in perfect peace,
> for it is trusting in You.
> ⁴ Trust in the Lord forever,
> because in Yah, the Lord, is an everlasting rock!
> ⁵ For He has humbled those who live in lofty places—
> an inaccessible city.
> He brings it down; He brings it down to the ground;
> He throws it to the dust.
> ⁶ Feet trample it,
> the feet of the humble,
> the steps of the poor.

### GOD'S PEOPLE VINDICATED

> *⁷ The path of the righteous is level;*
> *You clear a straight path for the righteous.*

> ⁸ Yes, Yahweh, we wait for You
> in the path of Your judgments.
> Our desire is for Your name and renown.
> ⁹ I long for You in the night;
> yes, my spirit within me diligently seeks You,
> for when Your judgments are in the land,
> the inhabitants of the world will learn righteousness.
> ¹⁰ But if the wicked man is shown favor,
> he does not learn righteousness.
> In a righteous land he acts unjustly
> and does not see the majesty of the Lord.

> ¹¹ Lord, Your hand is lifted up to take action,
> but they do not see it.
> They will see Your zeal for Your people,
> and they will be put to shame.
> The fire for Your adversaries will consume them!

¹² Lord, You will establish peace for us,
for You have also done all our work for us.
¹³ Yahweh our God, lords other than You have ruled over us,
but we remember Your name alone.

¹⁴ The dead do not live;
departed spirits do not rise up.
Indeed, You have visited and destroyed them;
You have wiped out all memory of them.
¹⁵ You have added to the nation, Lord.
You have added to the nation; You are honored.
You have expanded all the borders of the land.
¹⁶ Lord, they went to You in their distress;
they poured out whispered prayers
because Your discipline fell on them.
¹⁷ As a pregnant woman about to give birth
writhes and cries out in her pains,
so we were before You, Lord.
¹⁸ We became pregnant, we writhed in pain;
we gave birth to wind.
We have won no victories on earth,
and the earth's inhabitants have not fallen.

¹⁹ Your dead will live; their bodies will rise.
Awake and sing, you who dwell in the dust!
For you will be covered with the morning dew,
and the earth will bring out the departed spirits.

²⁰ Go, my people, enter your rooms
and close your doors behind you.
Hide for a little while until the wrath has passed.
²¹ For look, the Lord is coming from His place
to punish the inhabitants of the earth for their iniquity.
The earth will reveal the blood shed on it
and will no longer conceal her slain.

## ISAIAH 27

LEVIATHAN SLAIN

¹ On that day the Lord with His harsh, great, and strong sword, will bring judgment on Leviathan, the fleeing serpent—Leviathan, the twisting serpent. He will slay the monster that is in the sea.

THE LORD'S VINEYARD

² On that day
sing about a desirable vineyard:
³ I, Yahweh, watch over it;
I water it regularly.
I guard it night and day
so that no one disturbs it.
⁴ I am not angry,
but if it produces thorns and briers for Me,
I will fight against it, trample it,
and burn it to the ground.
⁵ Or let it take hold of My strength;
let it make peace with Me—
make peace with Me.
⁶ In days to come, Jacob will take root.
Israel will blossom and bloom
and fill the whole world with fruit.

⁷ Did the Lord strike Israel
as He struck the one who struck Israel?
Was he killed like those killed by Him?
⁸ You disputed with her
by banishing and driving her away.
He removed her with His severe storm
on the day of the east wind.
⁹ Therefore Jacob's iniquity will be purged in this way,
and the result of the removal of his sin will be this:
when he makes all the altar stones
like crushed bits of chalk,
no Asherah poles or incense altars will remain standing.
¹⁰ For the fortified city will be deserted,
pastures abandoned and forsaken like a wilderness.
Calves will graze there,
and there they will spread out and strip its branches.
¹¹ When its branches dry out, they will be broken off.
Women will come and make fires with them,
for they are not a people with understanding.
Therefore their Maker will not have compassion on them,
and their Creator will not be gracious to them.

¹² On that day
the Lord will thresh grain from the Euphrates River
as far as the Wadi of Egypt,
and you Israelites will be gathered one by one.

# GOD my KING

[13] On that day
a great trumpet will be blown,
and those lost in the land of Assyria will come,
as well as those dispersed in the land of Egypt;
and they will worship the Lord
at Jerusalem on the holy mountain.

**PSALM 74:12-17**

[12] God my King is from ancient times,
performing saving acts on the earth.
[13] You divided the sea with Your strength;
You smashed the heads of the sea monsters in the waters;
[14] You crushed the heads of Leviathan;
You fed him to the creatures of the desert.
[15] You opened up springs and streams;
You dried up ever-flowing rivers.
[16] The day is Yours, also the night;
You established the moon and the sun.
[17] You set all the boundaries of the earth;
You made summer and winter.

**PHILIPPIANS 4:4-7**

[4] Rejoice in the Lord always. I will say it again: Rejoice! [5] Let your graciousness be known to everyone. The Lord is near. [6] Don't worry about anything, but in everything, through prayer and petition with thanksgiving, let your requests be made known to God. [7] And the peace of God, which surpasses every thought, will guard your hearts and minds in Christ Jesus.

NOTES

DATE    /    /

<sup>DAY</sup> *20*

# GRACE
## *day*

Take this day as an opportunity to catch up on your reading, pray, and rest in the presence of the Lord.

*The day is Yours,
also the night;
You established the
moon and the sun.
You set all the boundaries
of the earth;
You made summer
and winter.*

PSALM 74:16-17

SERVES *4*

# BANANA NUT PORRIDGE

INGREDIENTS:

½ cup raw cashews
½ cup raw almonds
½ cup raw pecans
1 very ripe banana
2 cups coconut milk
2 teaspoons cinnamon
dash of sea salt for soaking water

INSTRUCTIONS:

Place the nuts in a large bowl and sprinkle the sea
salt over them. Fill the bowl with filtered water
so the nuts are covered by at least 1 inch of water.
Cover and soak overnight.

Drain the nuts and rinse 2 or 3 times, until the
water runs clear.

Add the drained nuts to a food processor or high-
speed blender. Blend the nuts with the banana,
coconut milk, and cinnamon until smooth.

Divide it into bowls and microwave for 40 seconds,
or put all of the porridge in a pot on the stove and
heat over medium-high heat for 5 minutes.

Serve with raisins, chopped nuts, and an extra
splash of milk if desired.

*DAY* **21**

# *weekly*
# TRUTH

Memorizing Scripture is one of the best ways to carry God-breathed truth, instruction, and reproof wherever we go.

In our Lenten study of Isaiah, we are memorizing Scripture about God's calling, judgment, and restoration of His people.

*For You have been a
stronghold for the poor,
a stronghold for the needy
person in his distress,
a refuge from the rain,
a shade from the heat.*

ISAIAH 25:4a

*Emily Jeffords, Coming Storm, 2013, oil, 30x40, Private Collection*

# 22

## *Who Is Worthy?*

*/ WEEK FOUR*

### WOE TO SAMARIA

¹ Woe to the majestic crown of Ephraim's drunkards,
and to the fading flower of its beautiful splendor,
which is on the summit above the rich valley.
Woe to those overcome with wine.
² Look, the Lord has a strong and mighty one—
like a devastating hail storm,
like a storm with strong flooding waters.
He will bring it across the land with His hand.
³ The majestic crown of Ephraim's drunkards
will be trampled underfoot.
⁴ The fading flower of his beautiful splendor,
which is on the summit above the rich valley,
will be like a ripe fig before the summer harvest.
Whoever sees it will swallow it
while it is still in his hand.
⁵ On that day
the Lord of Hosts will become a crown of beauty
and a diadem of splendor
to the remnant of His people,
⁶ a spirit of justice
to the one who sits in judgment,
and strength
to those who turn back the battle at the gate.

⁷ These also stagger because of wine
and stumble under the influence of beer:
priest and prophet stagger because of beer,
they are confused by wine.
They stumble because of beer,
they are muddled in their visions,
they stumble in their judgments.
⁸ Indeed, all their tables are covered with vomit;
there is no place without a stench.
⁹ Who is he trying to teach?
Who is he trying to instruct?
Infants just weaned from milk?
Babies removed from the breast?
¹⁰ For he says: "Law after law, law after law,
line after line, line after line,
a little here, a little there."
¹¹ So He will speak to this people
with stammering speech

and in a foreign language.
[12] He had said to them:
"This is the place of rest,
let the weary rest;
this is the place of repose."
But they would not listen.

[13] Then the word of the Lord came to them:
"Law after law, law after law,
line after line, line after line,
a little here, a little there,"
so they go stumbling backward,
to be broken, trapped, and captured.

# A precious CORNERSTONE

### A DEAL WITH DEATH

[14] Therefore hear the word of the Lord, you mockers
who rule this people in Jerusalem.
[15] For you said, "We have cut a deal with Death,
and we have made an agreement with Sheol;
when the overwhelming scourge passes through,
it will not touch us,
because we have made falsehood our refuge
and have hidden behind treachery."
[16] Therefore the Lord God said:
"Look, I have laid a stone in Zion,
a tested stone,
a precious cornerstone, a sure foundation;
the one who believes will be unshakable.
[17] And I will make justice the measuring line
and righteousness the mason's level."
Hail will sweep away the false refuge,
and water will flood your hiding place.
[18] Your deal with Death will be dissolved,
and your agreement with Sheol will not last.

When the overwhelming scourge passes through,
you will be trampled.
[19] Every time it passes through,
it will carry you away;
it will pass through every morning—
every day and every night.
Only terror will cause you
to understand the message.
[20] Indeed, the bed is too short to stretch out on,
and its cover too small to wrap up in.
[21] For the Lord will rise up as He did at Mount Perazim.
He will rise in wrath, as at the Valley of Gibeon,
to do His work, His strange work,
and to perform His task, His disturbing task.
[22] So now, do not mock,
or your shackles will become stronger.
Indeed, I have heard from the Lord God of Hosts
a decree of destruction for the whole land.

### GOD'S WONDERFUL ADVICE

[23] Listen and hear my voice.
Pay attention and hear what I say.
[24] Does the plowman plow every day to plant seed?
Does he continuously break up and cultivate the soil?
[25] When he has leveled its surface,
does he not then scatter black cumin and sow cumin?
He plants wheat in rows and barley in plots,
with spelt as their border.
[26] His God teaches him order;
He instructs him.
[27] Certainly black cumin is not threshed
with a threshing board,
and a cart wheel is not rolled over the cumin.
But black cumin is beaten out with a stick,
and cumin with a rod.
[28] Bread grain is crushed,
but is not threshed endlessly.
Though the wheel of the farmer's cart rumbles,
his horses do not crush it.
[29] This also comes from the Lord of Hosts.
He gives wonderful advice;
He gives great wisdom.

## ISAIAH 29

WOE TO JERUSALEM

[1] Woe to Ariel, Ariel,

the city where David camped!

Continue year after year;

let the festivals recur.

[2] I will oppress Ariel,

and there will be mourning and crying,

and she will be to Me like an Ariel.

[3] I will camp in a circle around you;

I will besiege you with earth ramps,

and I will set up my siege towers against you.

[4] You will be brought down;

you will speak from the ground,

and your words will come from low in the dust.

Your voice will be like that of a spirit from the ground;

your speech will whisper from the dust.

[5] Your many foes will be like fine dust,

and many of the ruthless, like blowing chaff.

Then suddenly, in an instant,

[6] you will be visited by the Lord of Hosts

with thunder, earthquake, and loud noise,

storm, tempest, and a flame of consuming fire.

[7] All the many nations

going out to battle against Ariel—

all the attackers, the siege works against her,

and those who oppress her—

will then be like a dream, a vision in the night.

[8] *It will be like a hungry one who dreams he is eating,*
*then wakes and is still hungry;*
*and like a thirsty one who dreams he is drinking,*
*then wakes and is still thirsty, longing for water.*
*So it will be for all the many nations*
*who go to battle against Mount Zion.*

I can't READ it, because IT IS sealed.

[9] Stop and be astonished;
blind yourselves and be blind!
They are drunk, but not with wine;
they stagger, but not with beer.
[10] For the Lord has poured out on you
an overwhelming urge to sleep;
He has shut your eyes—the prophets,
and covered your heads—the seers.

[11] For you the entire vision will be like the words of a sealed document. If it is given to one who can read and he is asked to read it, he will say, "I can't read it, because it is sealed." [12] And if the document is given to one who cannot read and he is asked to read it, he will say, "I can't read."

[13] The Lord said:

Because these people approach Me with their mouths
to honor Me with lip-service—
yet their hearts are far from Me,
and their worship consists of man-made rules
learned by rote—
[14] therefore I will again confound these people
with wonder after wonder.
The wisdom of their wise men will vanish,
and the understanding of the perceptive will be hidden.

[15] Woe to those who go to great lengths
to hide their plans from the Lord.
They do their works in darkness,
and say, "Who sees us? Who knows us?"
[16] You have turned things around,
as if the potter were the same as the clay.
How can what is made say about its maker,
"He didn't make me"?
How can what is formed
say about the one who formed it,
"He doesn't understand what he's doing"?

[17] Isn't it true that in just a little while
Lebanon will become an orchard,
and the orchard will seem like a forest?
[18] On that day the deaf will hear
the words of a document,
and out of a deep darkness
the eyes of the blind will see.
[19] The humble will have joy
after joy in the Lord,
and the poor people will rejoice
in the Holy One of Israel.
[20] For the ruthless one will vanish,
the scorner will disappear,
and all those who lie in wait with evil intent
will be killed—
[21] those who, with their speech,
accuse a person of wrongdoing,
who set a trap at the gate for the mediator,
and without cause deprive the righteous of justice.

[22] Therefore, the Lord who redeemed Abraham says this about the house of Jacob:

Jacob will no longer be ashamed
and his face will no longer be pale.
[23] For when he sees his children,
the work of My hands within his nation,
they will honor My name,
they will honor the Holy One of Jacob
and stand in awe of the God of Israel.
[24] Those who are confused will gain understanding,
and those who grumble will accept instruction.

## REVELATION 5

THE LAMB TAKES THE SCROLL

[1] Then I saw in the right hand of the One seated on the throne a scroll with writing on the inside and on the back, sealed with seven seals. [2] I also saw a mighty angel proclaiming in a loud voice,

*"Who is worthy to open the scroll and break its seals?"*

[3] But no one in heaven or on earth or under the earth was able to open the scroll or even to look in it. [4] And I cried and cried because no one was found worthy to open the scroll or even to look in it.

[5] Then one of the elders said to me, "Stop crying. Look! The Lion from the tribe of Judah, the Root of David, has been victorious so that He may open the scroll and its seven seals." [6] Then I saw One like a slaughtered lamb standing between the throne and the four living creatures and among the elders. He had seven horns and seven eyes, which are the seven spirits of God sent into all the earth. [7] He came and took the scroll out of the right hand of the One seated on the throne.

THE LAMB IS WORTHY

[8] When He took the scroll, the four living creatures and the 24 elders fell down before the Lamb. Each one had a harp and gold bowls filled with incense, which are the prayers of the saints. [9] And they sang a new song:

> You are worthy to take the scroll
> and to open its seals,
> because You were slaughtered,
> and You redeemed people
> for God by Your blood
> from every tribe and language
> and people and nation.
> [10] You made them a kingdom
> and priests to our God,
> and they will reign on the earth.

[11] Then I looked and heard the voice of many angels around the throne, and also of the living creatures and of the elders. Their number was countless thousands, plus thousands of thousands. [12] They said with a loud voice:

> The Lamb who was slaughtered is worthy
> to receive power and riches
> and wisdom and strength
> and honor and glory and blessing!

[13] I heard every creature in heaven, on earth, under the earth, on the sea, and everything in them say:

> Blessing and honor and glory and dominion
> to the One seated on the throne,
> and to the Lamb, forever and ever!

[14] The four living creatures said, "Amen," and the elders fell down and worshiped.

NOTES

DATE        /        /

# 23

## *The Lord's Mercy*

## ISAIAH 30

CONDEMNATION OF THE EGYPTIAN ALLIANCE

<sup>1</sup> Woe to the rebellious children!

This is the Lord's declaration.

They carry out a plan, but not Mine;
they make an alliance,
but against My will,
piling sin on top of sin.
<sup>2</sup> They set out to go down to Egypt
without asking My advice,
in order to seek shelter under Pharaoh's protection
and take refuge in Egypt's shadow.
<sup>3</sup> But Pharaoh's protection will become your shame,
and refuge in Egypt's shadow your disgrace.
<sup>4</sup> For though his princes are at Zoan
and his messengers reach as far as Hanes,
<sup>5</sup> everyone will be ashamed
because of a people who can't help.
They are of no benefit, they are no help;
they are good for nothing but shame and reproach.

<sup>6</sup> An oracle about the animals of the Negev:

Through a land of trouble and distress,
of lioness and lion,
of viper and flying serpent,
they carry their wealth on the backs of donkeys
and their treasures on the humps of camels,
to a people who will not help them.
<sup>7</sup> Egypt's help is completely worthless;
therefore, I call her:
Rahab Who Just Sits.

<sup>8</sup> Go now, write it on a tablet in their presence
and inscribe it on a scroll;
it will be for the future,
forever and ever.
<sup>9</sup> They are a rebellious people,
deceptive children,
children who do not want to obey the Lord's instruction.
<sup>10</sup> They say to the seers, "Do not see,"
and to the prophets,
"Do not prophesy the truth to us.
Tell us flattering things.
Prophesy illusions.

<sup>11</sup> Get out of the way!
Leave the pathway.
Rid us of the Holy One of Israel."
<sup>12</sup> Therefore the Holy One of Israel says:
"Because you have rejected this message
and have trusted in oppression and deceit,
and have depended on them,
<sup>13</sup> this iniquity of yours will be
like a spreading breach,
a bulge in a high wall
whose collapse will come in an instant—suddenly!
<sup>14</sup> Its collapse will be like the shattering
of a potter's jar, crushed to pieces,
so that not even a fragment of pottery
will be found among its shattered remains—
no fragment large enough to take fire from a hearth
or scoop water from a cistern."
<sup>15</sup> For the Lord God, the Holy One of Israel, has said:
"You will be delivered by returning and resting;
your strength will lie in quiet confidence.
But you are not willing."
<sup>16</sup> You say, "No!
We will escape on horses"—
therefore you will escape!—
and, "We will ride on fast horses"—
but those who pursue you will be faster.
<sup>17</sup> One thousand will flee at the threat of one,
at the threat of five you will flee,
until you alone remain
like a solitary pole on a mountaintop
or a banner on a hill.

**for the LORD is a just GOD.**

### THE LORD'S MERCY TO ISRAEL

<sup>18</sup> Therefore the Lord is waiting to show you mercy,
and is rising up to show you compassion,
for the Lord is a just God.
All who wait patiently for Him are happy.

<sup>19</sup> For you people will live on Zion in Jerusalem and will never cry again. He will show favor to you at the sound of your cry; when He hears, He will answer you. <sup>20</sup> The Lord will give you meager bread and water during oppression, but your Teacher will not hide Himself any longer. Your eyes will see your Teacher, <sup>21</sup> and whenever you turn to the right or to the left, your ears will hear this command behind you: "This is the way. Walk in it." <sup>22</sup> Then you will defile your silver-plated idols and your gold-plated images. You will throw them away like menstrual cloths, and call them filth.

<sup>23</sup> Then He will send rain for your seed that you have sown in the ground, and the food, the produce of the ground, will be rich and plentiful. On that day your cattle will graze in open pastures. <sup>24</sup> The oxen and donkeys that work the ground will eat salted fodder scattered with winnowing shovel and fork. <sup>25</sup> Streams flowing with water will be on every high mountain and every raised hill on the day of great slaughter when the towers fall. <sup>26</sup> The moonlight will be as bright as the sunlight, and the sunlight will be seven times brighter—like the light of seven days—on the day that the Lord bandages His people's injuries and heals the wounds He inflicted.

### ANNIHILATION OF THE ASSYRIANS

<sup>27</sup> Look, Yahweh comes from far away,
His anger burning and heavy with smoke.
His lips are full of fury,
and His tongue is like a consuming fire.
<sup>28</sup> His breath is like an overflowing torrent
that rises to the neck.
He comes to sift the nations in a sieve of destruction
and to put a bridle on the jaws of the peoples
to lead them astray.
<sup>29</sup> Your singing will be like that
on the night of a holy festival,
and your heart will rejoice

like one who walks to the music of a flute,

going up to the mountain of the Lord,

to the Rock of Israel.

30 And the Lord will make the splendor of His voice heard

and reveal His arm striking in angry wrath

and a flame of consuming fire,

in driving rain, a torrent, and hailstones.

31 Assyria will be shattered by the voice of the Lord.

He will strike with a rod.

32 And every stroke of the appointed staff

that the Lord brings down on him

will be to the sound of tambourines and lyres;

He will fight against him with brandished weapons.

33 Indeed! Topheth has been ready

for the king for a long time now.

Its funeral pyre is deep and wide,

with plenty of fire and wood.

The breath of the Lord, like a torrent of brimstone,

kindles it.

## JEREMIAH 31:31-34

### THE NEW COVENANT

31 "Look, the days are coming"—this is the Lord's declaration—"when I will make a new covenant with the house of Israel and with the house of Judah. 32 This one will not be like the covenant I made with their ancestors when I took them by the hand to bring them out of the land of Egypt—a covenant they broke even though I had married them"—the Lord's declaration. 33 "Instead, this is the covenant I will make with the house of Israel after those days"—the Lord's declaration. "I will put My teaching within them and write it on their hearts. I will be their God, and they will be My people. 34 No longer will one teach his neighbor or his brother, saying, 'Know the Lord,' for they will all know Me, from the least to the greatest of them"—this is the Lord's declaration. "For I will forgive their wrongdoing and never again remember their sin."

## ROMANS 8:14

*All those led by God's Spirit are God's sons.*

NOTES

DATE      /      /

# 24

## *Our Only Help*

¹ Woe to those who go down to Egypt for help
and who depend on horses!
They trust in the abundance of chariots
and in the large number of horsemen.
They do not look to the Holy One of Israel
and they do not seek the Lord's help.
² But He also is wise and brings disaster.
He does not go back on what He says;
He will rise up against the house of wicked men
and against the allies of evildoers.

³ *Egyptians are men, not God;*
*their horses are flesh, not spirit.*

When the Lord raises His hand to strike,
the helper will stumble
and the one who is helped will fall;
both will perish together.

⁴ For this is what the Lord said to me:

As a lion or young lion growls over its prey
when a band of shepherds is called out against it,
and is not terrified by their shouting
or subdued by their noise,
so the Lord of Hosts will come down
to fight on Mount Zion
and on its hill.
⁵ Like hovering birds,
so the Lord of Hosts will protect Jerusalem—
by protecting it, He will rescue it,
by sparing it, He will deliver it.

⁶ Return to the One the Israelites have greatly rebelled against. ⁷ For on that day, every one of you will reject the silver and gold idols that your own hands have sinfully made.

⁸ Then Assyria will fall,
but not by human sword;
a sword will devour him,
but not one made by man.

He will flee from the sword;
his young men will be put to forced labor.
⁹ His rock will pass away because of fear,
and his officers will be afraid because of the signal flag.

This is the Lord's declaration—whose fire is in Zion and whose furnace is in Jerusalem.

## ISAIAH 32

THE RIGHTEOUS KINGDOM ANNOUNCED

¹ Indeed, a king will reign righteously,
and rulers will rule justly.
² Each will be like a shelter from the wind,
a refuge from the rain,
like streams of water in a dry land
and the shade of a massive rock in an arid land.
³ Then the eyes of those who see will not be closed,
and the ears of those who hear will listen.
⁴ The reckless mind will gain knowledge,
and the stammering tongue will speak clearly and fluently.
⁵ A fool will no longer be called a noble,
nor a scoundrel said to be important.
⁶ For a fool speaks foolishness
and his mind plots iniquity.
He lives in a godless way
and speaks falsely about the Lord.
He leaves the hungry empty
and deprives the thirsty of drink.

⁷ *The scoundrel's weapons are destructive;*
*he hatches plots to destroy the needy with lies,*
*even when the poor says what is right.*
⁸ *But a noble person plans noble things;*
*he stands up for noble causes.*

⁹ Stand up, you complacent women;
listen to me.
Pay attention to what I say,
you overconfident daughters.

¹⁰ In a little more than a year
you overconfident ones will shudder,
for the vintage will fail
and the harvest will not come.
¹¹ Shudder, you complacent ones;
tremble, you overconfident ones!
Strip yourselves bare
and put sackcloth around your waists.
¹² Beat your breasts in mourning
for the delightful fields and the fruitful vines,
¹³ for the ground of my people
growing thorns and briers,
indeed, for every joyous house in the joyful city.
¹⁴ For the palace will be forsaken,
the busy city abandoned.
The hill and the watchtower will become
barren places forever,
the joy of wild donkeys,
and a pasture for flocks,
¹⁵ until the Spirit from heaven is poured out on us.
Then the desert will become an orchard,
and the orchard will seem like a forest.
¹⁶ Then justice will inhabit the wilderness,
and righteousness will dwell in the orchard.
¹⁷ The result of righteousness will be peace;
the effect of righteousness
will be quiet confidence forever.
¹⁸ Then my people will dwell in a peaceful place,
in safe and secure dwellings.
¹⁹ But hail will level the forest,
and the city will sink into the depths.
²⁰ Those who sow seed are happy
beside abundant waters;
they let ox and donkey range freely.

## PSALM 147:10-11

¹⁰ He is not impressed by the strength of a horse;
He does not value the power of a man.
¹¹ The Lord values those who fear Him,
those who put their hope in His faithful love.

# as the Lord PROMISED

## JOEL 2:28-32

GOD'S PROMISE OF HIS SPIRIT

[28] After this
I will pour out My Spirit on all humanity;
then your sons and your daughters will prophesy,
your old men will have dreams,
and your young men will see visions.
[29] I will even pour out My Spirit
on the male and female slaves in those days.
[30] I will display wonders
in the heavens and on the earth:
blood, fire, and columns of smoke.
[31] The sun will be turned to darkness
and the moon to blood
before the great and awe-inspiring Day of the Lord comes.
[32] Then everyone who calls
on the name of Yahweh will be saved,
for there will be an escape
for those on Mount Zion and in Jerusalem,
as the Lord promised,
among the survivors the Lord calls.

NOTES

DATE      /      /

## The Lord Rises Up

*/ WEEK FOUR*

¹ Woe, you destroyer never destroyed,
you traitor never betrayed!
When you have finished destroying,
you will be destroyed.
When you have finished betraying,
they will betray you.

² Lord, be gracious to us! We wait for You.
Be our strength every morning
and our salvation in time of trouble.
³ The peoples flee at the thunderous noise;
the nations scatter when You rise in Your majesty.
⁴ Your spoil will be gathered as locusts are gathered;
people will swarm over it like an infestation of locusts.
⁵ The Lord is exalted, for He dwells on high;
He has filled Zion with justice and righteousness.
⁶ There will be times of security for you—
a storehouse of salvation, wisdom, and knowledge.
The fear of the Lord is Zion's treasure.

⁷ Listen! Their warriors cry loudly in the streets;
the messengers of peace weep bitterly.
⁸ The highways are deserted;
travel has ceased.
An agreement has been broken,
cities despised,
and human life disregarded.
⁹ The land mourns and withers;
Lebanon is ashamed and decayed.
Sharon is like a desert;
Bashan and Carmel shake off their leaves.
¹⁰ "Now I will rise up," says the Lord.
"Now I will lift Myself up.
Now I will be exalted.
¹¹ You will conceive chaff;
you will give birth to stubble.
Your breath is fire that will consume you.
¹² The peoples will be burned to ashes,
like thorns cut down and burned in a fire.
¹³ You who are far off, hear what I have done;
you who are near, know My strength."

# SEE the KING in His beauty

<sup>14</sup> The sinners in Zion are afraid;
trembling seizes the ungodly:
"Who among us can dwell with a consuming fire?
Who among us can dwell with ever-burning flames?"
<sup>15</sup> The one who lives righteously
and speaks rightly,
who refuses gain from extortion,
whose hand never takes a bribe,
who stops his ears from listening to murderous plots
and shuts his eyes to avoid endorsing evil—
<sup>16</sup> he will dwell on the heights;
his refuge will be the rocky fortresses,
his food provided, his water assured.

<sup>17</sup> Your eyes will see the King in His beauty;
you will see a vast land.
<sup>18</sup> Your mind will meditate on the past terror:
"Where is the accountant?
Where is the tribute collector?
Where is the one who spied out our defenses?"
<sup>19</sup> You will no longer see the barbarians,
a people whose speech is difficult to comprehend—
who stammer in a language that is not understood.
<sup>20</sup> Look at Zion, the city of our festival times.
Your eyes will see Jerusalem,
a peaceful pasture, a tent that does not wander;
its tent pegs will not be pulled up
nor will any of its cords be loosened.
<sup>21</sup> For the majestic One, our Lord, will be there,
a place of rivers and broad streams
where ships that are rowed will not go,
and majestic vessels will not pass.
<sup>22</sup> For the Lord is our Judge,
the Lord is our lawgiver,
the Lord is our King.
He will save us.

<sup>23</sup> Your ropes are slack;
they cannot hold the base of the mast
or spread out the flag.
Then abundant spoil will be divided,
the lame will plunder it,
<sup>24</sup> and none there will say, "I am sick."

*The people who dwell there
will be forgiven their iniquity.*

## ISAIAH 34
### THE JUDGMENT OF THE NATIONS

<sup>1</sup> You nations, come here and listen;
you peoples, pay attention!
Let the earth hear, and all that fills it,
the world and all that comes from it.
<sup>2</sup> The Lord is angry with all the nations—
furious with all their armies.
He will set them apart for destruction,
giving them over to slaughter.
<sup>3</sup> Their slain will be thrown out,
and the stench of their corpses will rise;
the mountains will flow with their blood.
<sup>4</sup> All the heavenly bodies will dissolve.
The skies will roll up like a scroll,
and their stars will all wither
as leaves wither on the vine,
and foliage on the fig tree.

### THE JUDGMENT OF EDOM

<sup>5</sup> When My sword has drunk its fill in the heavens,
it will then come down on Edom
and on the people I have set apart for destruction.
<sup>6</sup> The Lord's sword is covered with blood.
It drips with fat,
with the blood of lambs and goats,
with the fat of the kidneys of rams.
For the Lord has a sacrifice in Bozrah,
a great slaughter in the land of Edom.
<sup>7</sup> The wild oxen will be struck down with them,
and young bulls with the mighty bulls.
Their land will be soaked with blood,
and their soil will be saturated with fat.

[8] For the Lord has a day of vengeance,
a time of paying back Edom
for its hostility against Zion.
[9] Edom's streams will be turned into pitch,
her soil into sulfur;
her land will become burning pitch.
[10] It will never go out—day or night.
Its smoke will go up forever.
It will be desolate, from generation to generation;
no one will pass through it forever and ever.
[11] The desert owl and the screech owl will possess it,
and the great owl and the raven will dwell there.
The Lord will stretch out a measuring line
and a plumb line over her
for her destruction and chaos.
[12] No nobles will be left to proclaim a king,
and all her princes will come to nothing.
[13] Her palaces will be overgrown with thorns;
her fortified cities, with thistles and briers.
She will become a dwelling for jackals,
an abode for ostriches.
[14] The desert creatures will meet hyenas,
and one wild goat will call to another.
Indeed, the screech owl will stay there
and will find a resting place for herself.
[15] The sand partridge will make her nest there;
she will lay and hatch her eggs
and will gather her brood under her shadow.
Indeed, the birds of prey will gather there,
each with its mate.
[16] Search and read the scroll of the Lord:
Not one of them will be missing,
none will be lacking its mate,
because He has ordered it by my mouth,
and He will gather them by His Spirit.
[17] He has ordained a lot for them;
His hand allotted their portion with a measuring line.
They will possess it forever;
they will dwell in it from generation to generation.

**2 CORINTHIANS 5:21**

He made the One who did not know sin to be sin for us, so that we might become the righteousness of God in Him.

**HEBREWS 12:28-29**

[28] Therefore, since we are receiving a kingdom that cannot be shaken, let us hold on to grace. By it, we may serve God acceptably, with reverence and awe, [29] for our God is a consuming fire.

NOTES

DATE      /      /

# The Ransomed Return to Zion

*/ WEEK FOUR*

¹ The wilderness and the dry land will be glad;
the desert will rejoice and blossom like a rose.
² It will blossom abundantly
and will also rejoice with joy and singing.
The glory of Lebanon will be given to it,
the splendor of Carmel and Sharon.
They will see the glory of the Lord,
the splendor of our God.
³ Strengthen the weak hands,
steady the shaking knees!
⁴ Say to the cowardly:
"Be strong; do not fear!
Here is your God; vengeance is coming.
God's retribution is coming; He will save you."
⁵ Then the eyes of the blind will be opened,
and the ears of the deaf unstopped.
⁶ Then the lame will leap like a deer,
and the tongue of the mute will sing for joy,
for water will gush in the wilderness,
and streams in the desert;
⁷ the parched ground will become a pool of water,
and the thirsty land springs of water.
In the haunt of jackals, in their lairs,
there will be grass, reeds, and papyrus.
⁸ A road will be there and a way;
it will be called the Holy Way.
The unclean will not travel on it,
but it will be for the one who walks the path.
Even the fool will not go astray.
⁹ There will be no lion there,
and no vicious beast will go up on it;
they will not be found there.
But the redeemed will walk on it,
¹⁰ and the redeemed of the Lord will return
and come to Zion with singing,
crowned with unending joy.
Joy and gladness will overtake them,
and sorrow and sighing will flee.

## ISAIAH 36

SENNACHERIB'S INVASION

¹ In the fourteenth year of King Hezekiah, Sennacherib king of Assyria attacked all the fortified cities of Judah and captured them. ² Then the king of Assyria sent the Rabshakeh, along with a massive army, from Lachish to King Hezekiah at Jerusalem. The Assyrian stood near the conduit of the upper pool, by the road to the Fuller's Field. ³ Eliakim son of Hilkiah, who was in charge of the palace, Shebna the court secretary, and Joah son of Asaph, the court historian, came out to him.

⁴ The Rabshakeh said to them, "Tell Hezekiah:

The great king, the king of Assyria, says this: What are you relying on? ⁵ I say that your strategy and military preparedness are mere words. What are you now relying on that you have rebelled against me? ⁶ Look, you are trusting in Egypt, that splintered reed of a staff that will enter and pierce the hand of anyone who leans on it. This is how Pharaoh king of Egypt is to all who trust in him. ⁷ Suppose you say to me, 'We trust in the Lord our God.' Isn't He the One whose high places and altars Hezekiah has removed, saying to Judah and Jerusalem, 'You are to worship at this altar'?

⁸ Now make a deal with my master, the king of Assyria. I'll give you 2,000 horses if you're able to supply riders for them! ⁹ How then can you drive back a single officer among the weakest of my master's officers and trust in Egypt for chariots and horsemen? ¹⁰ Have I attacked this land to destroy it without the Lord's approval? The Lord said to me, 'Attack this land and destroy it.'"

¹¹ Then Eliakim, Shebna, and Joah said to the Rabshakeh, "Please speak to your servants in Aramaic, since we understand it. Don't speak to us in Hebrew within earshot of the people who are on the wall."

¹² But the Rabshakeh replied, "Has my master sent me to speak these words to your master and to you, and not to the men who are sitting on the wall, who are destined with you to eat their own excrement and drink their own urine?"

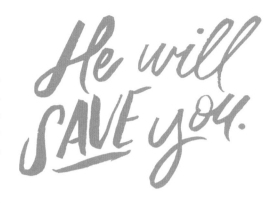

¹³ Then the Rabshakeh stood and called out loudly in Hebrew:

Listen to the words of the great king, the king of Assyria! ¹⁴ This is what the king says: "Don't let Hezekiah deceive you, for he cannot deliver you. ¹⁵ Don't let Hezekiah persuade you to trust in the Lord, saying, 'The Lord will certainly deliver us! This city will not be handed over to the king of Assyria.'"

¹⁶ Don't listen to Hezekiah, for this is what the king of Assyria says: "Make peace with me and surrender to me. Then every one of you may eat from his own vine and his own fig tree and drink water from his own cistern ¹⁷ until I come and take you away to a land like your own land—a land of grain and new wine, a land of bread and vineyards. ¹⁸ Beware that Hezekiah does not mislead you by saying, 'The Lord will deliver us.' Has any one of the gods of the nations delivered his land from the power of the king of Assyria? ¹⁹ Where are the gods of Hamath and Arpad? Where are the gods of Sepharvaim? Have they delivered Samaria from my power? ²⁰ Who among all the gods of these lands ever delivered his land from my power? So will the Lord deliver Jerusalem."

²¹ But they kept silent; they didn't say anything, for the king's command was, "Don't answer him." ²² Then Eliakim son of Hilkiah, who was in charge of the palace, Shebna the court secretary, and Joah son of Asaph, the court historian, came to Hezekiah with their clothes torn and reported to him the words of the Rabshakeh.

**HEBREWS 12:14**

*Pursue peace with everyone, and holiness—*
*without it no one will see the Lord.*

**REVELATION 21:4**

He will wipe away every tear from their eyes.
Death will no longer exist;
grief, crying, and pain will exist no longer,
because the previous things have passed away.

NOTES

*DAY* **27**

# GRACE
# *day*

Take this day as an opportunity to catch up on your reading, pray, and rest in the presence of the Lord.

*Therefore, since we are receiving a kingdom that cannot be shaken, let us hold on to grace. By it, we may serve God acceptably, with reverence and awe, for our God is a consuming fire.*

HEBREWS 12:28-29

SERVES *5*

# CHICKEN SOUP WITH ROASTED VEGETABLES

INGREDIENTS:

2 garlic cloves, minced
2 carrots, peeled and cubed
1 cup butternut squash, peeled and cubed
1 small sweet potato, peeled and cubed
½ yellow onion, quartered
2 tablespoons extra virgin olive oil
4 cups chicken stock, store-bought or homemade
2-3 cups shredded chicken
¾ teaspoon dried parsley
1 teaspoon sea salt
½ teaspoon dried thyme
½ teaspoon dried rosemary
¼ teaspoon dried oregano
¼ teaspoon cracked pepper
1 cup water
2 cups baby spinach

INSTRUCTIONS:

Preheat oven to 425°F.

Toss the vegetables in the olive oil and sprinkle with salt and pepper. Roast for 20 minutes, until the vegetables are tender.

Meanwhile, bring the chicken stock to a simmer in a large stockpot. Add the chicken, herbs, salt, and pepper. Cover and cook while the vegetables are roasting, about 15 minutes.

Add half the vegetables to the soup, and place the other half in a blender. Make sure to put all of the onion quarters into the blender. Puree the vegetables with the 1 cup of water.

Add the vegetable puree and baby spinach to the soup. Simmer for 5-10 minutes, until the spinach is wilted and the soup is hot. Adjust seasonings to your taste.

*DAY* **28**

# *weekly* TRUTH

Memorizing Scripture is one of the best ways to carry God-breathed truth, instruction, and reproof wherever we go.

In our Lenten study of Isaiah, we are memorizing Scripture about God's calling, judgment, and restoration of His people.

*He will destroy death forever.*
*The Lord God will wipe away*
*the tears from every face*
*and remove His people's disgrace*
*from the whole earth,*
*for the Lord has spoken.*
ISAIAH 25:8

*Emily Jeffords, Morning Blooms No. 3, 2015, oil, 4X4, Private Collection*

# 29

## Hezekiah's Prayer

### HEZEKIAH SEEKS ISAIAH'S COUNSEL

[1] When King Hezekiah heard their report, he tore his clothes, put on sackcloth, and went to the Lord's temple. [2] Then he sent Eliakim, who was in charge of the palace, Shebna the court secretary, and the leading priests, who were wearing sackcloth, to the prophet Isaiah son of Amoz. [3] They said to him, "This is what Hezekiah says: 'Today is a day of distress, rebuke, and disgrace, for children have come to the point of birth, and there is no strength to deliver them. [4] Perhaps Yahweh your God will hear all the words of the Rabshakeh, whom his master the king of Assyria sent to mock the living God, and will rebuke him for the words that Yahweh your God has heard. Therefore offer a prayer for the surviving remnant.'"

[5] So the servants of King Hezekiah went to Isaiah, [6] who said to them, "Tell your master this, 'The Lord says: Don't be afraid because of the words you have heard, which the king of Assyria's attendants have blasphemed Me with. [7] I am about to put a spirit in him and he will hear a rumor and return to his own land, where I will cause him to fall by the sword.'"

### SENNACHERIB'S LETTER

[8] When the Rabshakeh heard that the king of Assyria had left Lachish, he returned and found him fighting against Libnah. [9] The king had heard this about Tirhakah king of Cush: "He has set out to fight against you." So when he heard this, he sent messengers to Hezekiah, saying, [10] "Say this to Hezekiah king of Judah: 'Don't let your God, whom you trust, deceive you by promising that Jerusalem won't be handed over to the king of Assyria. [11] Look, you have heard what the kings of Assyria have done to all the countries: they completely destroyed them. Will you be rescued? [12] Did the gods of the nations that my predecessors destroyed rescue them—Gozan, Haran, Rezeph, and the Edenites in Telassar? [13] Where is the king of Hamath, the king of Arpad, the king of the city of Sepharvaim, Hena, or Ivvah?'"

HEZEKIAH'S PRAYER

¹⁴ Hezekiah took the letter from the messengers, read it, then went up to the Lord's temple and spread it out before the Lord. ¹⁵ Then Hezekiah prayed to the Lord:

¹⁶ Lord of Hosts, God of Israel, who is enthroned above the cherubim, You are God—You alone—of all the kingdoms of the earth. You made the heavens and the earth. ¹⁷ Listen closely, Lord, and hear; open Your eyes, Lord, and see. Hear all the words that Sennacherib has sent to mock the living God. ¹⁸ Lord, it is true that the kings of Assyria have devastated all these countries and their lands. ¹⁹ They have thrown their gods into the fire, for they were not gods but made by human hands—wood and stone. So they have destroyed them. ²⁰ Now, Lord our God, save us from his power so that all the kingdoms of the earth may know that You are the Lord—You alone.

GOD'S ANSWER THROUGH HEZEKIAH

²¹ Then Isaiah son of Amoz sent a message to Hezekiah: "The Lord, the God of Israel, says: 'Because you prayed to Me about Sennacherib king of Assyria, ²² this is the word the Lord has spoken against him:

Virgin Daughter Zion
despises you and scorns you:
Daughter Jerusalem shakes her head
behind your back.
²³ Who is it you have mocked and blasphemed?
Who have you raised your voice against
and lifted your eyes in pride?
Against the Holy One of Israel!
²⁴ You have mocked the Lord through your servants.
You have said, "With my many chariots
I have gone up to the heights of the mountains,
to the far recesses of Lebanon.
I cut down its tallest cedars,
its choice cypress trees.
I came to its distant heights,
its densest forest.
²⁵ I dug wells and drank water.
I dried up all the streams of Egypt
with the soles of my feet."

²⁶ Have you not heard?
I designed it long ago;
I planned it in days gone by.
I have now brought it to pass,
and you have crushed fortified cities
into piles of rubble.
²⁷ Their inhabitants have become powerless,
dismayed, and ashamed.
They are plants of the field,
tender grass,
grass on the rooftops,
blasted by the east wind.

²⁸ But I know your sitting down,
your going out and your coming in,
and your raging against Me.
²⁹ Because your raging against Me
and your arrogance have reached My ears,
I will put My hook in your nose
and My bit in your mouth;
I will make you go back
the way you came.

³⁰ "'This will be the sign for you: This year you will eat what grows on its own, and in the second year what grows from that. But in the third year sow and reap, plant vineyards and eat their fruit. ³¹ The surviving remnant of the house of Judah will again take root downward and bear fruit upward. ³² For a remnant will go out from Jerusalem and survivors, from Mount Zion. The zeal of the Lord of Hosts will accomplish this.'

³³ "Therefore, this is what the Lord says about the king of Assyria:

He will not enter this city
or shoot an arrow there
or come before it with a shield
or build up an assault ramp against it.
³⁴ He will go back
the way he came,
and he will not enter this city.
This is the Lord's declaration.

*Continued*

# CROWN HIM WITH MANY CROWNS

TEXT: MATTHEW BRIDGES, 1851    TUNE: GEORGE J. ELVEY

1 Crown Him with ma - ny crowns, the Lamb up - on His throne.
2 Crown Him the Lord of life, who tri - umphed o'er the grave,
3 Crown Him the Lord of love; be - hold His hands and side,
4 Crown Him the Lord of years, the po - ten - tate of time,

Hark! how the heaven - ly an - them drowns all mu - sic but its own.
and rose vic - to - rious in the strife for those He came to save;
rich wounds, yet vi - si - ble a - bove, in beau - ty glo - ri - fied;
cre - a - tor of the rol - ling spheres, in - ef - fa - bly su - blime.

A - wake, my soul, and sing of Him who died for thee,
His glo - ries now we sing who died and rose on high,
no an - gels in the sky can ful - ly bear that sight,
All hail, Re - dee - mer, hail! for Thou hast died for me;

and hail Him as thy match - less king through all e - ter - ni - ty.
who died e - ter - nal life to bring, and lives that death may die.
but down - ward bends their bur - ning eye at my - ste - ries so bright.
Thy praise shall ne - ver, ne - ver fail through - out e - ter - ni - ty.

*35 I will defend this city and rescue it
because of Me
and because of My servant David."*

### DEFEAT AND DEATH OF SENNACHERIB

36 Then the angel of the Lord went out and struck down 185,000 in the camp of the Assyrians. When the people got up the next morning—there were all the dead bodies! 37 So Sennacherib king of Assyria broke camp and left. He returned home and lived in Nineveh.

38 One day, while he was worshiping in the temple of his god Nisroch, his sons Adrammelech and Sharezer struck him down with the sword and escaped to the land of Ararat. Then his son Esar-haddon became king in his place.

## ISAIAH 38

### HEZEKIAH'S ILLNESS AND RECOVERY

1 In those days Hezekiah became terminally ill. The prophet Isaiah son of Amoz came and said to him, "This is what the Lord says: 'Put your affairs in order, for you are about to die; you will not recover.'"

2 Then Hezekiah turned his face to the wall and prayed to the Lord. 3 He said, "Please, Lord, remember how I have walked before You faithfully and wholeheartedly, and have done what pleases You." And Hezekiah wept bitterly.

4 Then the word of the Lord came to Isaiah: 5 "Go and tell Hezekiah that this is what the Lord God of your ancestor David says: I have heard your prayer; I have seen your tears. Look, I am going to add 15 years to your life. 6 And I will deliver you and this city from the power of the king of Assyria; I will defend this city. 7 This is the sign to you from the Lord that He will do what He has promised: 8 I am going to make the sun's shadow that goes down on Ahaz's stairway go back by 10 steps." So the sun's shadow went back the 10 steps it had descended.

9 A poem by Hezekiah king of Judah after he had been sick and had recovered from his illness:

10 I said: In the prime of my life
I must go to the gates of Sheol;
I am deprived of the rest of my years.
11 I said: I will never see the Lord,
the Lord in the land of the living;
I will not look on humanity any longer
with the inhabitants of what is passing away.
12 My dwelling is plucked up and removed from me
like a shepherd's tent.
I have rolled up my life like a weaver;
He cuts me off from the loom.
You make an end of me from day until night.
13 I thought until the morning:
He will break all my bones like a lion;
You make an end of me day and night.
14 I chirp like a swallow or a crane;
I moan like a dove.
My eyes grow weak looking upward.
Lord, I am oppressed; support me.

15 What can I say?
He has spoken to me,
and He Himself has done it.
I walk along slowly all my years
because of the bitterness of my soul,
16 Lord, because of these promises people live,
and in all of them is the life of my spirit as well;
You have restored me to health
and let me live.
17 Indeed, it was for my own welfare
that I had such great bitterness;
but Your love has delivered me
from the Pit of destruction,
for You have thrown all my sins behind Your back.
18 For Sheol cannot thank You;
Death cannot praise You.
Those who go down to the Pit
cannot hope for Your faithfulness.
19 The living, only the living can thank You,
as I do today;
a father will make Your faithfulness known to children.
20 The Lord will save me;
we will play stringed instruments
all the days of our lives
at the house of the Lord.

²¹ Now Isaiah had said, "Let them take a lump of pressed figs and apply it to his infected skin, so that he may recover." ²² And Hezekiah had asked, "What is the sign that I will go up to the Lord's temple?"

## ISAIAH 39
### HEZEKIAH'S FOLLY

¹ At that time Merodach-baladan son of Baladan, king of Babylon, sent letters and a gift to Hezekiah since he heard that he had been sick and had recovered. ² Hezekiah was pleased with them, and showed them his treasure house—the silver, the gold, the spices, and the precious oil—and all his armory, and everything that was found in his treasuries. There was nothing in his palace and in all his realm that Hezekiah did not show them.

³ Then the prophet Isaiah came to King Hezekiah and asked him, "Where did these men come from and what did they say to you?"

Hezekiah replied, "They came to me from a distant country, from Babylon."

⁴ Isaiah asked, "What have they seen in your palace?"

Hezekiah answered, "They have seen everything in my palace. There isn't anything in my treasuries that I didn't show them."

⁵ Then Isaiah said to Hezekiah, "Hear the word of the Lord of Hosts: ⁶ 'The time will certainly come when everything in your palace and all that your fathers have stored up until this day will be carried off to Babylon; nothing will be left,' says the Lord. ⁷ 'Some of your descendants who come from you will be taken away, and they will become eunuchs in the palace of the king of Babylon.'"

⁸ Then Hezekiah said to Isaiah, "The word of the Lord that you have spoken is good," for he thought: There will be peace and security during my lifetime.

## PSALM 30:1-3
### JOY IN THE MORNING

*A psalm; a dedication song for the house. Davidic.*

¹ I will exalt You, Lord,
because You have lifted me up
and have not allowed my enemies
to triumph over me.
² Lord my God,
I cried to You for help, and You healed me.
³ Lord, You brought me up from Sheol;
You spared me from among those
going down to the Pit.

## MICAH 7:18-20

¹⁸ Who is a God like You,
removing iniquity and passing over rebellion
for the remnant of His inheritance?
He does not hold on to His anger forever,
because He delights in faithful love.
¹⁹ He will again have compassion on us;
He will vanquish our iniquities.
You will cast all our sins
into the depths of the sea.
²⁰ You will show loyalty to Jacob
and faithful love to Abraham,
as You swore to our fathers
from days long ago.

into the depths OF THE SEA.

NOTES

DATE    /    /

# 30

## God's People Comforted

GOD'S PEOPLE COMFORTED

¹ "Comfort, comfort My people,"
says your God.
² "Speak tenderly to Jerusalem,
and announce to her
that her time of forced labor is over,
her iniquity has been pardoned,
and she has received from the Lord's hand
double for all her sins."

³ A voice of one crying out:

Prepare the way of the Lord in the wilderness;
make a straight highway for our God in the desert.
⁴ Every valley will be lifted up,
and every mountain and hill will be leveled;
the uneven ground will become smooth
and the rough places, a plain.
⁵ And the glory of the Lord will appear,
and all humanity together will see it,
for the mouth of the Lord has spoken.

⁶ A voice was saying, "Cry out!"
Another said, "What should I cry out?"
"All humanity is grass,
and all its goodness is like the flower of the field.
⁷ The grass withers, the flowers fade
when the breath of the Lord blows on them;
indeed, the people are grass.
⁸ The grass withers, the flowers fade,
but the word of our God remains forever."

⁹ Zion, herald of good news,
go up on a high mountain.
Jerusalem, herald of good news,
raise your voice loudly.
Raise it, do not be afraid!
Say to the cities of Judah,
"Here is your God!"
¹⁰ See, the Lord God comes with strength,
and His power establishes His rule.
His reward is with Him,
and His gifts accompany Him.

11 He protects His flock like a shepherd;
He gathers the lambs in His arms
and carries them in the fold of His garment.
He gently leads those that are nursing.

12 Who has measured the waters in the hollow of his hand
or marked off the heavens with the span of his hand?
Who has gathered the dust of the earth in a measure
or weighed the mountains in a balance
and the hills in the scales?
13 Who has directed the Spirit of the Lord,
or who gave Him His counsel?
14 Who did He consult with?
Who gave Him understanding
and taught Him the paths of justice?
Who taught Him knowledge
and showed Him the way of understanding?
15 Look, the nations are like a drop in a bucket;
they are considered as a speck of dust in the scales;
He lifts up the islands like fine dust.
16 Lebanon is not enough for fuel,
or its animals enough for a burnt offering.
17 All the nations are as nothing before Him;
they are considered by Him
as nothingness and emptiness.

18 Who will you compare God with?
What likeness will you compare Him to?
19 To an idol?—something that a smelter casts,
and a metalworker plates with gold
and makes silver welds for it?
20 To one who shapes a pedestal,
choosing wood that does not rot?
He looks for a skilled craftsman
to set up an idol that will not fall over.

21 Do you not know?
Have you not heard?
Has it not been declared to you
from the beginning?
Have you not considered
the foundations of the earth

22 God is enthroned above the circle of the earth;
its inhabitants are like grasshoppers.

He stretches out the heavens like thin cloth
and spreads them out like a tent to live in.
23 He reduces princes to nothing
and makes judges of the earth irrational.
24 They are barely planted, barely sown,
their stem hardly takes root in the ground
when He blows on them and they wither,
and a whirlwind carries them away like stubble.

25 "Who will you compare Me to,
or who is My equal?" asks the Holy One.
26 Look up and see:
who created these?
He brings out the starry host by number;
He calls all of them by name.
Because of His great power and strength,
not one of them is missing.

27 Jacob, why do you say,
and Israel, why do you assert:
"My way is hidden from the Lord,
and my claim is ignored by my God"?
28 Do you not know?
Have you not heard?
Yahweh is the everlasting God,
the Creator of the whole earth.
He never grows faint or weary;
there is no limit to His understanding.
29 He gives strength to the weary
and strengthens the powerless.
30 Youths may faint and grow weary,
and young men stumble and fall,
31 but those who trust in the Lord
will renew their strength;
they will soar on wings like eagles;
they will run and not grow weary;
they will walk and not faint.

THE grass WITHERS AND THE flowers FADE

## ISAIAH 41

### THE LORD VERSUS THE NATIONS' GODS

[1] "Be silent before Me, islands!
And let peoples renew their strength.
Let them approach, then let them testify;
let us come together for the trial.
[2] Who has stirred him up from the east?
He calls righteousness to his feet.
The Lord hands nations over to him,
and he subdues kings.
He makes them like dust with his sword,
like wind-driven stubble with his bow.
[3] He pursues them, going on safely,
hardly touching the path with his feet.
[4] Who has performed and done this,
calling the generations from the beginning?
I, Yahweh, am the first,
and with the last—I am He."

[5] The islands see and are afraid,
the whole earth trembles.
They approach and arrive.
[6] Each one helps the other,
and says to another, "Take courage!"
[7] The craftsman encourages the metalworker;
the one who flattens with the hammer
supports the one who strikes the anvil,
saying of the soldering, "It is good."
He fastens it with nails so that it will not fall over.

[8] But you, Israel, My servant,
Jacob, whom I have chosen,
descendant of Abraham, My friend—
[9] I brought you from the ends of the earth
and called you from its farthest corners.
I said to you: You are My servant;
I have chosen you and not rejected you.
[10] Do not fear, for I am with you;
do not be afraid, for I am your God.
I will strengthen you; I will help you;
I will hold on to you with My righteous right hand.

SOAR on wings like EAGLES

11 Be sure that all who are enraged against you
will be ashamed and disgraced;
those who contend with you
will become as nothing and will perish.
12 You will look for those who contend with you,
but you will not find them.
Those who war against you
will become absolutely nothing.
13 For I, Yahweh your God,
hold your right hand
and say to you: Do not fear,
I will help you.
14 Do not fear, you worm Jacob,
you men of Israel:
I will help you—
                                this is the Lord's declaration.
Your Redeemer is the Holy One of Israel.
15 See, I will make you into a sharp threshing board,
new, with many teeth.
You will thresh mountains and pulverize them
and make hills into chaff.
16 You will winnow them
and a wind will carry them away,
a gale will scatter them.
But you will rejoice in the Lord;
you will boast in the Holy One of Israel.

17 The poor and the needy seek water, but there
is none;
their tongues are parched with thirst.
I, Yahweh, will answer them;
I, the God of Israel, will not forsake them.
18 I will open rivers on the barren heights,
and springs in the middle of the plains.
I will turn the desert into a pool of water
and dry land into springs of water.
19 I will plant cedars in the desert,
acacias, myrtles, and olive trees.
I will put juniper trees in the desert,
elms and cypress trees together,
20 so that all may see and know,
consider and understand,
that the hand of the Lord has done this,
the Holy One of Israel has created it.

21 "Submit your case," says the Lord.
"Present your arguments," says Jacob's King.
22 "Let them come and tell us
what will happen.
Tell us the past events,
so that we may reflect on them
and know the outcome,
or tell us the future.
23 Tell us the coming events,
then we will know that you are gods.
Indeed, do something good or bad,
then we will be in awe and perceive.
24 Look, you are nothing
and your work is worthless.
Anyone who chooses you is detestable.

25 "I have raised up one from the north, and he
has come,
one from the east who invokes My name.
He will march over rulers as if they were mud,
like a potter who treads the clay.
26 Who told about this from the beginning,
so that we might know,
and from times past,
so that we might say: He is right?
No one announced it,
no one told it,
no one heard your words.
27 I was the first to say to Zion:
Look! Here they are!
And I gave a herald of good news to Jerusalem.
28 When I look, there is no one;
there is no counselor among them;
when I ask them, they have nothing to say.
29 Look, all of them are a delusion;
their works are nonexistent;
their images are wind and emptiness."

## JOHN 1:23

*He said, "I am a voice of one crying out in
the wilderness: Make straight the way of the
Lord—just as Isaiah the prophet said."*

## 2 CORINTHIANS 1:3-7

THE GOD OF COMFORT

[3] Praise the God and Father of our Lord Jesus Christ, the Father of mercies and the God of all comfort. [4] He comforts us in all our affliction, so that we may be able to comfort those who are in any kind of affliction, through the comfort we ourselves receive from God. [5] For as the sufferings of Christ overflow to us, so through Christ our comfort also overflows. [6] If we are afflicted, it is for your comfort and salvation. If we are comforted, it is for your comfort, which is experienced in your endurance of the same sufferings that we suffer. [7] And our hope for you is firm, because we know that as you share in the sufferings, so you will share in the comfort.

NOTES

DATE     /     /

# 31

## A Song of Praise

### THE SERVANT'S MISSION

[1] "This is My Servant; I strengthen Him,
this is My Chosen One; I delight in Him.
I have put My Spirit on Him;
He will bring justice to the nations.
[2] He will not cry out or shout
or make His voice heard in the streets.
[3] He will not break a bruised reed,
and He will not put out a smoldering wick;
He will faithfully bring justice.
[4] He will not grow weak or be discouraged
until He has established justice on earth.
The islands will wait for His instruction."

[5] This is what God, Yahweh, says—
who created the heavens and stretched them out,
who spread out the earth and what comes from it,
who gives breath to the people on it
and life to those who walk on it—
[6] "I, Yahweh, have called You
for a righteous purpose,
and I will hold You by Your hand.
I will keep You and appoint You
to be a covenant for the people
and a light to the nations,
[7] in order to open blind eyes,
to bring out prisoners from the dungeon,
and those sitting in darkness from the prison house.
[8] I am Yahweh, that is My name;
I will not give My glory to another
or My praise to idols.
[9] The past events have indeed happened.
Now I declare new events;
I announce them to you before they occur."

### A SONG OF PRAISE

[10] Sing a new song to the Lord;
sing His praise from the ends of the earth,
you who go down to the sea with all that fills it,
you islands with your inhabitants.
[11] Let the desert and its cities shout,
the settlements where Kedar dwells cry aloud.

Let the inhabitants of Sela sing for joy;
let them cry out from the mountaintops.
¹² Let them give glory to the Lord
and declare His praise in the islands.
¹³ The Lord advances like a warrior;
He stirs up His zeal like a soldier.
He shouts, He roars aloud,
He prevails over His enemies.

¹⁴ "I have kept silent from ages past;
I have been quiet and restrained Myself.
But now, I will groan like a woman in labor,
gasping breathlessly.
¹⁵ I will lay waste mountains and hills
and dry up all their vegetation.
I will turn rivers into islands
and dry up marshes.
¹⁶ I will lead the blind by a way they did not know;
I will guide them on paths they have not known.
I will turn darkness to light in front of them
and rough places into level ground.
This is what I will do for them,
and I will not forsake them.
¹⁷ They will be turned back and utterly ashamed—
those who trust in idols
and say to metal-plated images:
You are our gods!

### ISRAEL'S BLINDNESS AND DEAFNESS

¹⁸ "Listen, you deaf!
Look, you blind, so that you may see.
¹⁹ Who is blind but My servant,
or deaf like My messenger I am sending?
Who is blind like My dedicated one,
or blind like the servant of the Lord?
²⁰ Though seeing many things, you do not obey.
Though his ears are open, he does not listen."

²¹ The Lord was pleased, because of His righteousness,
to magnify His instruction and make it glorious.
²² But this is a people plundered and looted,
all of them trapped in holes
or imprisoned in dungeons.

They have become plunder
with no one to rescue them
and loot, with no one saying, "Give it back!"
²³ Who among you will pay attention to this?
Let him listen and obey in the future.
²⁴ Who gave Jacob to the robber,
and Israel to the plunderers?
Was it not the Lord?
Have we not sinned against Him?
They were not willing to walk in His ways,
and they would not listen to His instruction.
²⁵ So He poured out on Jacob His furious anger
and the power of war.
It surrounded him with fire, but he did not know it;
it burned him, but he paid no attention.

## ISAIAH 43

### RESTORATION OF ISRAEL

¹ Now this is what the Lord says—
the One who created you, Jacob,
and the One who formed you, Israel—
"Do not fear, for I have redeemed you;
I have called you by your name; you are Mine.
² I will be with you
when you pass through the waters,
and when you pass through the rivers,
they will not overwhelm you.
You will not be scorched
when you walk through the fire,
and the flame will not burn you.
³ For I Yahweh your God,
the Holy One of Israel, and your Savior,
give Egypt as a ransom for you,
Cush and Seba in your place.

⁴ Because you are precious in My sight
and honored, and I love you,
I will give people in exchange for you
and nations instead of your life.
⁵ Do not fear, for I am with you;
I will bring your descendants from the east,
and gather you from the west.
⁶ I will say to the north: Give them up!
and to the south: Do not hold them back!
Bring My sons from far away,
and My daughters from the ends of the earth—
⁷ everyone called by My name
and created for My glory.
I have formed him; indeed, I have made him."

⁸ Bring out a people who are blind, yet have eyes,
and are deaf, yet have ears.
⁹ All the nations are gathered together,
and the peoples are assembled.
Who among them can declare this,
and tell us the former things?
Let them present their witnesses
to vindicate themselves,
so that people may hear and say, "It is true."
¹⁰ "You are My witnesses"—
this is the Lord's declaration—
"and My servant whom I have chosen,
so that you may know and believe Me
and understand that I am He.
No god was formed before Me,
and there will be none after Me.
¹¹ I, I am Yahweh,
and there is no other Savior but Me.
¹² I alone declared, saved, and proclaimed—
and not some foreign god among you.
So you are My witnesses"—
this is the Lord's declaration—
"and I am God.
¹³ Also, from today on I am He alone,
and none can deliver from My hand.
I act, and who can reverse it?"

GOD'S DELIVERANCE OF REBELLIOUS ISRAEL

¹⁴ This is what the Lord, your Redeemer, the Holy One of Israel says:

Because of you, I will send to Babylon
and bring all of them as fugitives,
even the Chaldeans in the ships in which they rejoice.
¹⁵ I am Yahweh, your Holy One,
the Creator of Israel, your King.

¹⁶ This is what the Lord says—
who makes a way in the sea,
and a path through surging waters,
¹⁷ who brings out the chariot and horse,
the army and the mighty one together
(they lie down, they do not rise again;
they are extinguished, quenched like a wick)—
¹⁸ "Do not remember the past events,
pay no attention to things of old.
¹⁹ Look, I am about to do something new;
even now it is coming. Do you not see it?
Indeed, I will make a way in the wilderness,
rivers in the desert.
²⁰ The animals of the field will honor Me,
jackals and ostriches,
because I provide water in the wilderness,
and rivers in the desert,
to give drink to My chosen people.
²¹ The people I formed for Myself
will declare My praise.

²² "But Jacob, you have not called on Me,
because, Israel, you have become weary of Me.
²³ You have not brought Me your sheep for
burnt offerings
or honored Me with your sacrifices.
I have not burdened you with offerings
or wearied you with incense.

*²⁴ You have not bought Me aromatic cane*
  *with silver,*
*or satisfied Me with the fat of your sacrifices.*
*But you have burdened Me with your sins;*
*you have wearied Me with your iniquities.*

²⁵ "It is I who sweep away your transgressions

for My own sake

and remember your sins no more.

²⁶ Take Me to court; let us argue our case together.

State your case, so that you may be vindicated.

²⁷ Your first father sinned,

and your mediators have rebelled against Me.

²⁸ So I defiled the officers of the sanctuary,

and set Jacob apart for destruction

and Israel for abuse.

**PSALM 72:1-4**

A PRAYER FOR THE KING

*Solomonic.*

¹ God, give Your justice to the king

and Your righteousness to the king's son.

² He will judge Your people with righteousness

and Your afflicted ones with justice.

³ May the mountains bring prosperity to the people

and the hills, righteousness.

⁴ May he vindicate the afflicted among the people,

help the poor,

and crush the oppressor.

**2 CORINTHIANS 5:17**

Therefore, if anyone is in Christ, he is a new creation;
old things have passed away, and look, new things
have come.

# 32

## *There Is No Other God*

/ WEEK FIVE

SPIRITUAL BLESSING

¹ "And now listen, Jacob My servant,
Israel whom I have chosen.
² This is the word of the Lord
your Maker who formed you from the womb;
He will help you:
Do not fear; Jacob is My servant;
I have chosen Jeshurun.
³ For I will pour water on the thirsty land
and streams on the dry ground;
I will pour out My Spirit on your descendants
and My blessing on your offspring.
⁴ They will sprout among the grass
like poplars by flowing streams.
⁵ This one will say, 'I am the Lord's';
another will call himself by the name of Jacob;
still another will write on his hand, 'The Lord's,'
and name himself by the name of Israel."

NO GOD OTHER THAN YAHWEH

⁶ This is what the Lord, the King of Israel and its Redeemer,
the Lord of Hosts, says:

I am the first and I am the last.
There is no God but Me.
⁷ Who, like Me, can announce the future?
Let him say so and make a case before Me,
since I have established an ancient people.
Let these gods declare the coming things,
and what will take place.
⁸ Do not be startled or afraid.
Have I not told you and declared it long ago?
You are my witnesses!
Is there any God but Me?
There is no other Rock; I do not know any.

⁹ All who make idols are nothing,
and what they treasure does not profit.
Their witnesses do not see or know anything,
so they will be put to shame.
¹⁰ Who makes a god or casts a metal image
for no profit?

[11] Look, all its worshipers will be put to shame,
and the craftsmen are humans.
They all will assemble and stand;
they all will be startled and put to shame.

[12] The ironworker labors over the coals,
shapes the idol with hammers,
and works it with his strong arm.
Also he grows hungry and his strength fails;
he doesn't drink water and is faint.
[13] The woodworker stretches out a measuring line,
he outlines it with a stylus;
he shapes it with chisels
and outlines it with a compass.
He makes it according to a human likeness,
like a beautiful person,
to dwell in a temple.
[14] He cuts down cedars for his use,
or he takes a cypress or an oak.
He lets it grow strong among the trees of the forest.
He plants a laurel, and the rain makes it grow.
[15] It serves as fuel for man.
He takes some of it and warms himself;
also he kindles a fire and bakes bread;
he even makes it into a god and worships it;
he makes an idol from it and bows down to it.
[16] He burns half of it in a fire,
and he roasts meat on that half.
He eats the roast and is satisfied.
He warms himself and says, "Ah!
I am warm, I see the blaze."
[17] He makes a god or his idol with the rest of it.
He bows down to it and worships;
He prays to it, "Save me, for you are my god."
[18] Such people do not comprehend
and cannot understand,
for He has shut their eyes so they cannot see,
and their minds so they cannot understand.
[19] No one reflects,
no one has the perception or insight to say,
"I burned half of it in the fire,
I also baked bread on its coals,

I roasted meat and ate.
I will make something detestable with the rest of it,
and I will bow down to a block of wood."
[20] He feeds on ashes.
His deceived mind has led him astray,
and he cannot deliver himself,
or say, "Isn't there a lie in my right hand?"

[21] Remember these things, Jacob,
and Israel, for you are My servant;
I formed you, you are My servant;
Israel, you will never be forgotten by Me.
[22] I have swept away your transgressions like a cloud,
and your sins like a mist.
Return to Me,
for I have redeemed you.
[23] Rejoice, heavens, for the Lord has acted;
shout, depths of the earth.
Break out into singing, mountains,
forest, and every tree in it.
For the Lord has redeemed Jacob,
and glorifies Himself through Israel.

RESTORATION OF ISRAEL THROUGH CYRUS

[24] This is what the Lord, your Redeemer who formed you
from the womb, says:

I am Yahweh, who made everything;
who stretched out the heavens by Myself;
who alone spread out the earth;

<sup>25</sup> who destroys the omens of the false prophets
and makes fools of diviners;
who confounds the wise
and makes their knowledge foolishness;
<sup>26</sup> who confirms the message of His servant
and fulfills the counsel of His messengers;
who says to Jerusalem, "She will be inhabited,"
and to the cities of Judah, "They will be rebuilt,"
and I will restore her ruins;
<sup>27</sup> who says to the depths of the sea, "Be dry,"
and I will dry up your rivers;
<sup>28</sup> who says to Cyrus, "My shepherd,
he will fulfill all My pleasure"
and says to Jerusalem, "She will be rebuilt,"
and of the temple, "Its foundation will be laid."

## ISAIAH 45

<sup>1</sup> The Lord says this to Cyrus, His anointed,
whose right hand I have grasped
to subdue nations before him,
to disarm kings,
to open the doors before him
and the gates will not be shut:
<sup>2</sup> "I will go before you
and level the uneven places;
I will shatter the bronze doors
and cut the iron bars in two.
<sup>3</sup> I will give you the treasures of darkness
and riches from secret places,
so that you may know that I, Yahweh,
the God of Israel call you by your name.
<sup>4</sup> I call you by your name,
because of Jacob My servant
and Israel My chosen one.
I give a name to you,
though you do not know Me.
<sup>5</sup> I am Yahweh, and there is no other;
there is no God but Me.
I will strengthen you,
though you do not know Me,
<sup>6</sup> so that all may know from the rising of the
sun to its setting
that there is no one but Me.
I am Yahweh, and there is no other.

<sup>7</sup> I form light and create darkness,
I make success and create disaster;
I, Yahweh, do all these things.

<sup>8</sup> "Heavens, sprinkle from above,
and let the skies shower righteousness.
Let the earth open up
so that salvation will sprout
and righteousness will spring up with it.
I, Yahweh, have created it.

<sup>9</sup> *"Woe to the one who argues with*
   *his Maker—*
*one clay pot among many.*
*Does clay say to the one forming it,*
*'What are you making?'*
*Or does your work say,*
*'He has no hands'?*

<sup>10</sup> How absurd is the one who says to his father,
'What are you fathering?'
or to his mother,
'What are you giving birth to?'"
<sup>11</sup> This is what the Lord,
the Holy One of Israel and its Maker, says:
"Ask Me what is to happen to My sons,
and instruct Me about the work of My hands.
<sup>12</sup> I made the earth,
and created man on it.
It was My hands that stretched out the heavens,
and I commanded all their host.
<sup>13</sup> I have raised him up in righteousness,
and will level all roads for him.
He will rebuild My city,
and set My exiles free,
not for a price or a bribe,"
says the Lord of Hosts.

### GOD ALONE IS THE SAVIOR

<sup>14</sup> This is what the Lord says:

The products of Egypt and the merchandise of Cush
and the Sabeans, men of stature,

# EVERY knee will bow

will come over to you
and will be yours;
they will follow you,
they will come over in chains
and bow down to you.
They will confess to you:
God is indeed with you, and there is no other;
there is no other God.

[15] Yes, You are a God who hides Himself,
God of Israel, Savior.
[16] All of them are put to shame, even humiliated;
the makers of idols go in humiliation together.
[17] Israel will be saved by the Lord
with an everlasting salvation;
you will not be put to shame or humiliated
for all eternity.

[18] For this is what the Lord says—
God is the Creator of the heavens.
He formed the earth and made it.
He established it;
He did not create it to be empty,
but formed it to be inhabited—
"I am Yahweh,
and there is no other.
[19] I have not spoken in secret,
somewhere in a land of darkness.
I did not say to the descendants of Jacob:
Seek Me in a wasteland.

I, Yahweh, speak truthfully;
I say what is right.

[20] "Come, gather together,
and draw near, you fugitives of the nations.
Those who carry their wooden idols,
and pray to a god who cannot save,
have no knowledge.
[21] Speak up and present your case—
yes, let them take counsel together.
Who predicted this long ago?
Who announced it from ancient times?
Was it not I, Yahweh?
There is no other God but Me,
a righteous God and Savior;
there is no one except Me.
[22] Turn to Me and be saved,
all the ends of the earth.
For I am God,
and there is no other.
[23] By Myself I have sworn;
Truth has gone from My mouth,
a word that will not be revoked:
Every knee will bow to Me,
every tongue will swear allegiance.
[24] It will be said to Me: Righteousness and strength
is only in the Lord."
All who are enraged against Him
will come to Him and be put to shame.
[25] All the descendants of Israel
will be justified and find glory through the Lord.

**ROMANS 14:10-11**

[10] But you, why do you criticize your brother? Or you, why do you look down on your brother? For we will all stand before the tribunal of God. [11] For it is written:

*As I live, says the Lord,*
*every knee will bow to Me,*
*and every tongue will give praise to God.*

**REVELATION 22:12-13**

[12] "Look! I am coming quickly, and My reward is with Me to repay each person according to what he has done. [13] I am the Alpha and the Omega, the First and the Last, the Beginning and the End."

NOTES

DATE     /     /

# 33

## The Fall of Babylon

THERE IS NO ONE LIKE GOD

1 Bel crouches; Nebo cowers.
Their idols are consigned to beasts and cattle.
The images you carry are loaded,
as a burden for the weary animal.
2 The gods cower; they crouch together;
they are not able to rescue the burden,
but they themselves go into captivity.

3 "Listen to Me, house of Jacob,
all the remnant of the house of Israel,
who have been sustained from the womb,
carried along since birth.
4 I will be the same until your old age,
and I will bear you up when you turn gray.
I have made you, and I will carry you;
I will bear and save you.

5 "Who will you compare Me or make Me equal to?
Who will you measure Me with,
so that we should be like each other?
6 Those who pour out their bags of gold
and weigh out silver on scales—
they hire a goldsmith and he makes it into a god.
Then they kneel and bow down to it.
7 They lift it to their shoulder and bear it along;
they set it in its place, and there it stands;
it does not budge from its place.
They cry out to it but it doesn't answer;
it saves no one from his trouble.

8 "Remember this and be brave;
take it to heart, you transgressors!
9 Remember what happened long ago,
for I am God, and there is no other;
I am God, and no one is like Me.
10 I declare the end from the beginning,
and from long ago what is not yet done,
saying: My plan will take place,
and I will do all My will.
11 I call a bird of prey from the east,
a man for My purpose from a far country.
Yes, I have spoken; so I will also bring it about.
I have planned it; I will also do it.

¹² Listen to me, you hardhearted,
far removed from justice:
¹³ I am bringing My justice near;
it is not far away,
and My salvation will not delay.
I will put salvation in Zion,
My splendor in Israel.

## ISAIAH 47

THE FALL OF BABYLON

¹ "Go down and sit in the dust,
Virgin Daughter Babylon.
Sit on the ground without a throne,
Daughter Chaldea!
For you will no longer be called pampered and spoiled.
² Take millstones and grind meal;
remove your veil,
strip off your skirt, bare your thigh,
wade through the streams.
³ Your nakedness will be uncovered,
and your shame will be exposed.
I will take vengeance;
I will spare no one.
⁴ The Holy One of Israel is our Redeemer;
Yahweh of Hosts is His name.

⁵ "Daughter Chaldea,
sit in silence and go into darkness.
For you will no longer be called mistress of kingdoms.
⁶ I was angry with My people;
I profaned My possession,
and I placed them under your control.
You showed them no mercy;
you made your yoke very heavy on the elderly.
⁷ You said, 'I will be the mistress forever.'
You did not take these things to heart
or think about their outcome.

⁸ "So now hear this, lover of luxury,
who sits securely,
who says to herself,
'I exist, and there is no one else.
I will never be a widow
or know the loss of children.'
⁹ These two things will happen to you
suddenly, in one day:
loss of children and widowhood.
They will happen to you in their entirety,
in spite of your many sorceries
and the potency of your spells.
¹⁰ You were secure in your wickedness;
you said, 'No one sees me.'
Your wisdom and knowledge
led you astray.
You said to yourself,
'I exist, and there is no one else.'
¹¹ But disaster will happen to you;
you will not know how to avert it.
And it will fall on you,
but you will be unable to ward it off.
Devastation will happen to you suddenly
and unexpectedly.
¹² So take your stand with your spells
and your many sorceries,
which you have wearied yourself with from your youth.
Perhaps you will be able to succeed;
perhaps you will inspire terror!
¹³ You are worn out with your many consultations.
So let them stand and save you—
the astrologers, who observe the stars,
who predict monthly
what will happen to you.
¹⁴ Look, they are like stubble;
fire burns them up.
They cannot deliver themselves
from the power of the flame.
This is not a coal for warming themselves,
or a fire to sit beside!
¹⁵ This is what they are to you—
those who have wearied you
and have traded with you from your youth—
each wanders on his own way;
no one can save you."

**PSALM 71:17-19**

[17] God, You have taught me from my youth,
and I still proclaim Your wonderful works.
[18] Even when I am old and gray,
God, do not abandon me.
Then I will proclaim Your power
to another generation,
Your strength to all who are to come.
[19] Your righteousness reaches heaven, God,
You who have done great things;
God, who is like You?

**PROVERBS 19:21**

*Many plans are in a man's heart,*
*but the Lord's decree will prevail.*

NOTES

*34*

# GRACE
## *day*

Take this day as an opportunity to catch up on your reading, pray, and rest in the presence of the Lord.

*Your righteousness reaches heaven, God, You who have done great things; God, who is like You?*

PSALM 71:19

SERVES *4*

# SPIRALIZED ZUCCHINI PESTO PASTA WITH PEAS AND PANCETTA

### INGREDIENTS:

¼ pound pancetta, diced
4 large zucchini, spiralized
¼ cup pesto sauce
¼ teaspoon sea salt
pinch of fresh cracked pepper
½ cup frozen peas, thawed
¼ cup ricotta cheese

### INSTRUCTIONS:

Heat a large skillet over medium-high heat. Add the pancetta and cook for 5 to 7 minutes, until crisp.

Add the zucchini noodles and sauté for 5 minutes, until crisp-tender. Stir in the pesto and season with salt and pepper. Remove from heat and stir in the thawed peas.

Divide among serving dishes and top with crumbled cheese and a sprig of fresh basil.

*DAY* **35**

# *weekly* TRUTH

Memorizing Scripture is one of the best ways to carry God-breathed truth, instruction, and reproof wherever we go.

In our Lenten study of Isaiah, we are memorizing Scripture about God's calling, judgment, and restoration of His people. This week's passage is the key verse for the book of Isaiah.

*Now this is what the LORD says—*
*the One who created you, Jacob,*
*and the One who formed you, Israel—*
*"Do not fear, for I have redeemed you;*
*I have called you by your name; you*
*are Mine."*

ISAIAH 43:1

*Emily Jeffords, To The Stillness, 2013, oil, 16X20, Private Collection*

# 36

## *The Servant Brings Salvation*

ISRAEL MUST LEAVE BABYLON

¹ "Listen to this, house of Jacob—
those who are called by the name Israel
and have descended from Judah,
who swear by the name of Yahweh
and declare the God of Israel,
but not in truth or righteousness.
² For they are named after the Holy City,
and lean on the God of Israel;
His name is Yahweh of Hosts.
³ I declared the past events long ago;
they came out of My mouth; I proclaimed them.
Suddenly I acted, and they occurred.
⁴ Because I know that you are stubborn,
and your neck is iron
and your forehead bronze,
⁵ therefore I declared to you long ago.
I announced it to you before it occurred,
so you could not claim, 'My idol caused them;
my carved image and cast idol control them.'
⁶ You have heard it. Observe it all.
Will you not acknowledge it?
From now on I will announce new things to you,
hidden things that you have not known.
⁷ They have been created now, and not long ago;
you have not heard of them before today,
so you could not claim, 'I already knew them!'
⁸ You have never heard; you have never known;
For a long time your ears have not been open.
For I knew that you were very treacherous,
and were known as a rebel from birth.
⁹ I will delay My anger for the honor of My name,
and I will restrain Myself for your benefit and for
My praise,
so that you will not be destroyed.
¹⁰ Look, I have refined you, but not as silver;
I have tested you in the furnace of affliction.
¹¹ I will act for My own sake, indeed, My own,
for how can I be defiled?
I will not give My glory to another.

¹² "Listen to Me, Jacob,
and Israel, the one called by Me:

*I am He; I am the first,*
*I am also the last.*

¹³ My own hand founded the earth,
and My right hand spread out the heavens;
when I summoned them,
they stood up together.
¹⁴ All of you, assemble and listen!
Who among the idols has declared these things?
The Lord loves him;
he will accomplish His will against Babylon,
and His arm will be against the Chaldeans.
¹⁵ I—I have spoken;
yes, I have called him;
I have brought him,
and he will succeed in his mission.
¹⁶ Approach Me and listen to this.
From the beginning I have not spoken in secret;
from the time anything existed, I was there."
And now the Lord God
has sent me and His Spirit.

¹⁷ This is what the Lord, your Redeemer, the Holy One of Israel says:

I am Yahweh your God,
who teaches you for your benefit,
who leads you in the way you should go.
¹⁸ If only you had paid attention to My commands.
Then your peace would have been like a river,
and your righteousness like the waves of the sea.
¹⁹ Your descendants would have been as countless as the sand,
and the offspring of your body like its grains;
their name would not be cut off
or eliminated from My presence.

²⁰ Leave Babylon,
flee from the Chaldeans!
Declare with a shout of joy,
proclaim this,
let it go out to the end of the earth;
announce,
"The Lord has redeemed His servant Jacob!"

²¹ They did not thirst
when He led them through the deserts;
He made water flow for them from the rock;
He split the rock, and water gushed out.
²² "There is no peace for the wicked," says the Lord.

## ISAIAH 49

THE SERVANT BRINGS SALVATION

¹ Coastlands, listen to me;
distant peoples, pay attention.
The Lord called me before I was born.
He named me while I was in my mother's womb.
² He made my words like a sharp sword;
He hid me in the shadow of His hand.
He made me like a sharpened arrow;
He hid me in His quiver.
³ He said to me, "You are My Servant, Israel;
I will be glorified in him."
⁴ But I myself said: I have labored in vain,
I have spent my strength for nothing and futility;
yet my vindication is with the Lord,
and my reward is with my God.
⁵ And now, says the Lord,
who formed me from the womb to be His Servant,
to bring Jacob back to Him
so that Israel might be gathered to Him;
for I am honored in the sight of the Lord,
and my God is my strength—
⁶ He says,
"It is not enough for you to be My Servant
raising up the tribes of Jacob
and restoring the protected ones of Israel.
I will also make you a light for the nations,
to be My salvation to the ends of the earth."

[7] This is what the Lord,

the Redeemer of Israel, his Holy One, says

to one who is despised,

to one abhorred by people,

to a servant of rulers:

"Kings will see and stand up,

and princes will bow down,

because of the Lord, who is faithful,

the Holy One of Israel—and He has chosen you."

[8] This is what the Lord says:

I will answer you in a time of favor,

and I will help you in the day of salvation.

I will keep you, and I will appoint you

to be a covenant for the people,

to restore the land,

to make them possess the desolate inheritances,

[9] saying to the prisoners: Come out,

and to those who are in darkness: Show yourselves.

They will feed along the pathways,

and their pastures will be on all the barren heights.

[10] They will not hunger or thirst,

the scorching heat or sun will not strike them;

for their compassionate One will guide them,

and lead them to springs of water.

[11] I will make all My mountains into a road,

and My highways will be raised up.

[12] See, these will come from far away,

from the north and from the west,

and from the land of Sinim.

[13] *Shout for joy, you heavens!*
*Earth, rejoice!*
*Mountains break into joyful shouts!*
*For the Lord has comforted His people,*
*and will have compassion on His*
*    afflicted ones.*

ZION REMEMBERED

[14] Zion says, "The Lord has abandoned me;

The Lord has forgotten me!"

[15] "Can a woman forget her nursing child,

or lack compassion for the child of her womb?

Even if these forget,

yet I will not forget you.

[16] Look, I have inscribed you on the palms of My hands;

your walls are continually before Me.

[17] Your builders hurry;

those who destroy and devastate you will leave you.

[18] Look up, and look around.

They all gather together; they come to you.

As I live"—

this is the Lord's declaration—

"you will wear all your children as jewelry,

and put them on as a bride does.

[19] For your waste and desolate places

and your land marked by ruins—

will now be indeed too small for the inhabitants,

and those who swallowed you up will be far away.

[20] Yet as you listen, the children

that you have been deprived of will say,

'This place is too small for me;

make room for me so that I may settle.'

[21] Then you will say within yourself,

'Who fathered these for me?

I was deprived of my children and unable to conceive,

exiled and wandering—

but who brought them up?

See, I was left by myself—

but these, where did they come from?'"

[22] This is what the Lord God says:

Look, I will lift up My hand to the nations,

and raise My banner to the peoples.

They will bring your sons in their arms,

and your daughters will be carried on their shoulders.

[23] Kings will be your foster fathers,

and their queens your nursing mothers.

They will bow down to you

with their faces to the ground,

and lick the dust at your feet.

NOTES               DATE   /   /

Then you will know that I am Yahweh;
those who put their hope in Me
will not be put to shame.

[24] Can the prey be taken from the mighty,
or the captives of the righteous be delivered?
[25] For this is what the Lord says:
"Even the captives of a mighty man will be taken,
and the prey of a tyrant will be delivered;
I will contend with the one who contends with you,
and I will save your children.
[26] I will make your oppressors eat their own flesh,
and they will be drunk with their own blood
as with sweet wine.
Then all flesh will know
that I, Yahweh, am your Savior,
and your Redeemer, the Mighty One of Jacob."

## COLOSSIANS 1:13-14

[13] He has rescued us from the domain of darkness and transferred us into the kingdom of the Son He loves. [14] We have redemption, the forgiveness of sins, in Him.

## HEBREWS 4:12

For the word of God is living and effective and sharper than any double-edged sword, penetrating as far as the separation of soul and spirit, joints and marrow. It is able to judge the ideas and thoughts of the heart.

# THE OLD RUGGED CROSS

TEXT AND TUNE: GEORGE BERNARD, 1913

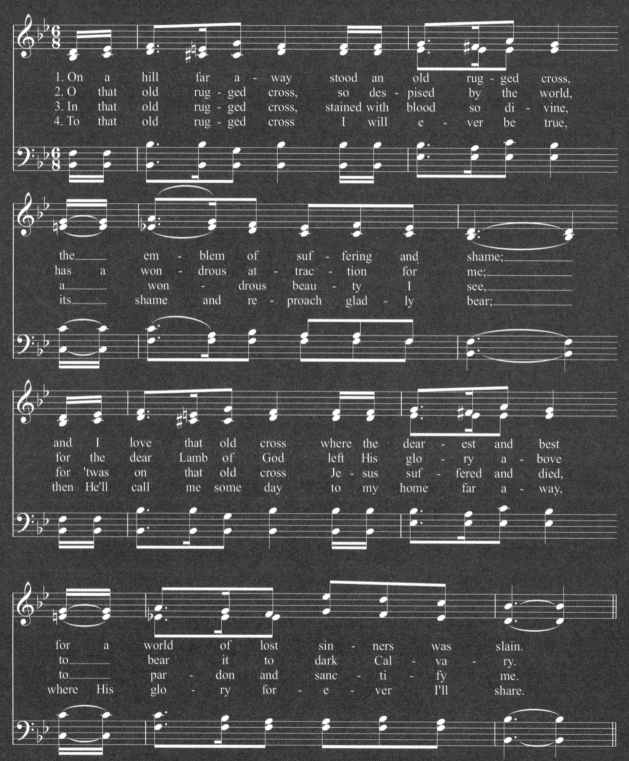

1. On a hill far a-way stood an old rug-ged cross,
2. O that old rug-ged cross, so des-pised by the world,
3. In that old rug-ged cross, stained with blood so di-vine,
4. To that old rug-ged cross I will e-ver be true,

the em-blem of suf-fering and shame;
has a won-drous at-trac-tion for me;
a won-drous beau-ty I see,
its shame and re-proach glad-ly bear;

and I love that old cross where the dear-est and best
for the dear Lamb of God left His glo-ry a-bove
for 'twas on that old cross Je-sus suf-fered and died,
then He'll call me some day to my home far a-way,

for a world of lost sin-ners was slain.
to bear it to dark Cal-va-ry.
to par-don and sanc-ti-fy me.
where His glo-ry for-e-ver I'll share.

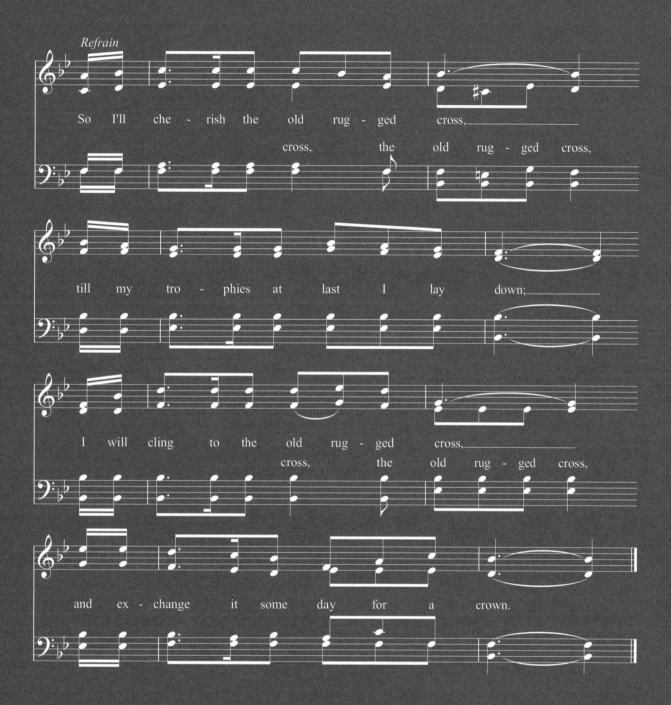

So I'll che - rish the old rug - ged cross,_____

cross, the old rug - ged cross,

till my tro - phies at last I lay down;_____

I will cling to the old rug - ged cross,_____

cross, the old rug - ged cross,

and ex - change it some day for a crown.

# 37

## The Lord Will Defend

/ WEEK SIX

¹ This is what the Lord says:

> Where is your mother's divorce certificate
> that I used to send her away?
> Or who were My creditors that I sold you to?
> Look, you were sold for your iniquities,
> and your mother was put away
> because of your transgressions.
> ² Why was no one there when I came?
> Why was there no one to answer when I called?
> Is My hand too short to redeem?
> Or do I have no power to deliver?
> Look, I dry up the sea by My rebuke;
> I turn the rivers into a wilderness;
> their fish rot because of lack of water
> and die of thirst.
> ³ I dress the heavens in black
> and make sackcloth their clothing.

### THE OBEDIENT SERVANT

> ⁴ The Lord God has given Me
> the tongue of those who are instructed
> to know how to sustain the weary with a word.
> He awakens Me each morning;
> He awakens My ear to listen like those being instructed.
> ⁵ The Lord God has opened My ear,
> and I was not rebellious;
> I did not turn back.
> ⁶ I gave My back to those who beat Me,
> and My cheeks to those who tore out My beard.
> I did not hide My face from scorn and spitting.
> ⁷ The Lord God will help Me;
> therefore I have not been humiliated;
> therefore I have set My face like flint,
> and I know I will not be put to shame.
> ⁸ The One who vindicates Me is near;
> who will contend with Me?
> Let us confront each other.
> Who has a case against Me?
> Let him come near Me!
> ⁹ In truth, the Lord God will help Me;
> who will condemn Me?
> Indeed, all of them will wear out like a garment;
> a moth will devour them.

*¹⁰ Who among you fears the Lord,*
*listening to the voice of His Servant?*
*Who among you walks in darkness,*
*and has no light?*
*Let him trust in the name of Yahweh;*
*let him lean on his God.*

¹¹ Look, all you who kindle a fire,
who encircle yourselves with firebrands;
walk in the light of your fire
and in the firebrands you have lit!
This is what you'll get from My hand:
you will lie down in a place of torment.

## ISAIAH 51

### SALVATION FOR ZION

¹ Listen to Me, you who pursue righteousness,
you who seek the Lord:
Look to the rock from which you were cut,
and to the quarry from which you were dug.
² Look to Abraham your father,
and to Sarah who gave birth to you in pain.
When I called him, he was only one;
I blessed him and made him many.
³ For the Lord will comfort Zion;
He will comfort all her waste places,
and He will make her wilderness like Eden,
and her desert like the garden of the Lord.
Joy and gladness will be found in her,
thanksgiving and melodious song.
⁴ Pay attention to Me, My people,
and listen to Me, My nation;
for instruction will come from Me,
and My justice for a light to the nations.
I will bring it about quickly.
⁵ My righteousness is near,
My salvation appears,
and My arms will bring justice to the nations.
The coastlands will put their hope in Me,
and they will look to My strength.
⁶ Look up to the heavens,
and look at the earth beneath;
for the heavens will vanish like smoke,

the earth will wear out like a garment,
and its inhabitants will die like gnats.
But My salvation will last forever,
and My righteousness will never be shattered.

⁷ Listen to Me, you who know righteousness,
the people in whose heart is My instruction:
do not fear disgrace by men,
and do not be shattered by their taunts.
⁸ For the moth will devour them like a garment,
and the worm will eat them like wool.
But My righteousness will last forever,
and My salvation for all generations.

⁹ Wake up, wake up!
Put on the strength of the Lord's power.
Wake up as in days past,
as in generations of long ago.
Wasn't it You who hacked Rahab to pieces,
who pierced the sea monster?
¹⁰ Wasn't it You who dried up the sea,
the waters of the great deep,
who made the sea-bed into a road
for the redeemed to pass over?
¹¹ And the redeemed of the Lord will return
and come to Zion with singing,
crowned with unending joy.
Joy and gladness will overtake them,
and sorrow and sighing will flee.

¹² I—I am the One who comforts you.
Who are you that you should fear man who dies,
or a son of man who is given up like grass?
¹³ But you have forgotten the Lord, your Maker,
who stretched out the heavens
and laid the foundations of the earth.
You are in constant dread all day long
because of the fury of the oppressor,
who has set himself to destroy.
But where is the fury of the oppressor?
¹⁴ The prisoner is soon to be set free;
he will not die and go to the Pit,
and his food will not be lacking.

[15] For I am Yahweh your God

who stirs up the sea so that its waves roar—

His name is Yahweh of Hosts.

[16] I have put My words in your mouth,

and covered you in the shadow of My hand,

in order to plant the heavens,

to found the earth,

and to say to Zion, "You are My people."


[17] Wake yourself, wake yourself up!

Stand up, Jerusalem,

you who have drunk the cup of His fury

from the hand of the Lord;

you who have drunk the goblet to the dregs—

the cup that causes people to stagger.

[18] There is no one to guide her

among all the children she has raised;

there is no one to take hold of her hand

among all the offspring she has brought up.

[19] These two things have happened to you:

devastation and destruction,

famine and sword.

Who will grieve for you?

How can I comfort you?

[20] Your children have fainted;

they lie at the head of every street

like an antelope in a net.

They are full of the Lord's fury,

the rebuke of your God.


[21] So listen to this, afflicted

and drunken one—but not with wine.

[22] This is what your Lord says—

Yahweh, even your God,

who defends His people—

"Look, I have removed

the cup of staggering from your hand;

that goblet, the cup of My fury.

You will never drink it again.

[23] I will put it into the hands of your tormentors,

who said to you:

Lie down, so we can walk over you.

You made your back like the ground,

and like a street for those who walk on it.

## ISAIAH 52

[1] "Wake up, wake up;

put on your strength, Zion!

Put on your beautiful garments,

Jerusalem, the Holy City!

For the uncircumcised and the unclean

will no longer enter you.

[2] Stand up, shake the dust off yourself!

Take your seat, Jerusalem.

Remove the bonds from your neck,

captive Daughter Zion."

[3] For this is what the Lord says:

"You were sold for nothing,

and you will be redeemed without silver."

[4] For this is what the Lord God says:

"At first My people went down to Egypt to live there,

then Assyria oppressed them without cause.

[5] So now what have I here"—

this is the Lord's declaration—

"that My people are taken away for nothing?

Its rulers wail"—

this is the Lord's declaration—

"and My name is continually blasphemed all day long.

[6] Therefore My people will know My name;

therefore they will know on that day

that I am He who says:

Here I am."


[7] How beautiful on the mountains

are the feet of the herald,

who proclaims peace,

who brings news of good things,

who proclaims salvation,

who says to Zion, "Your God reigns!"

[8] The voices of your watchmen—

they lift up their voices,

shouting for joy together;

for every eye will see

when the Lord returns to Zion.

[9] Be joyful, rejoice together,

you ruins of Jerusalem!

For the Lord has comforted His people;

He has redeemed Jerusalem.

[10] The Lord has displayed His holy arm

in the sight of all the nations;

all the ends of the earth will see
the salvation of our God.

_____

[11] Leave, leave, go out from there!
Do not touch anything unclean;
go out from her, purify yourselves,
you who carry the vessels of the Lord.
[12] For you will not leave in a hurry,
and you will not have to take flight;
because the Lord is going before you,
and the God of Israel is your rear guard.

### THE SERVANT'S SUFFERING AND EXALTATION

[13] See, My Servant will act wisely;
He will be raised and lifted up and greatly exalted.
[14] Just as many were appalled at You—
His appearance was so disfigured
that He did not look like a man,
and His form did not resemble a human being—
[15] so He will sprinkle many nations.
Kings will shut their mouths because of Him,
For they will see what had not been told them,
and they will understand what they had not heard.

### MATTHEW 27:26-31

[26] Then he released Barabbas to them. But after having Jesus flogged, he handed Him over to be crucified.

### MOCKED BY THE MILITARY

[27] Then the governor's soldiers took Jesus into headquarters and gathered the whole company around Him. [28] They stripped Him and dressed Him in a scarlet military robe. [29] They twisted together a crown of thorns, put it on His head, and placed a reed in His right hand. And they knelt down before Him and mocked Him: "Hail, King of the Jews!" [30] Then they spit on Him, took the reed, and kept hitting Him on the head. [31] When they had mocked Him, they stripped Him of the robe, put His clothes on Him, and led Him away to crucify Him.

### JOHN 16:33

"I have told you these things so that in Me you may have peace. You will have suffering in this world. Be courageous! I have conquered the world."

# 38

## Covenant of Peace

¹ Who has believed what we have heard?
And who has the arm of the Lord been revealed to?

² *He grew up before Him like a young plant*
*and like a root out of dry ground.*
*He didn't have an impressive form*
*or majesty that we should look at Him,*
*no appearance that we should desire Him.*

³ He was despised and rejected by men,
a man of suffering who knew what sickness was.
He was like someone people turned away from;
He was despised, and we didn't value Him.

⁴ Yet He Himself bore our sicknesses,
and He carried our pains;
but we in turn regarded Him stricken,
struck down by God, and afflicted.
⁵ But He was pierced because of our transgressions,
crushed because of our iniquities;
punishment for our peace was on Him,
and we are healed by His wounds.
⁶ We all went astray like sheep;
we all have turned to our own way;
and the Lord has punished Him
for the iniquity of us all.

⁷ He was oppressed and afflicted,
yet He did not open His mouth.
Like a lamb led to the slaughter
and like a sheep silent before her shearers,
He did not open His mouth.
⁸ He was taken away because of oppression and judgment;
and who considered His fate?
For He was cut off from the land of the living;
He was struck because of my people's rebellion.
⁹ They made His grave with the wicked
and with a rich man at His death,
although He had done no violence
and had not spoken deceitfully.

[10] Yet the Lord was pleased to crush Him severely.
When You make Him a restitution offering,
He will see His seed, He will prolong His days,
and by His hand, the Lord's pleasure will
be accomplished.
[11] He will see it out of His anguish,
and He will be satisfied with His knowledge.
My righteous Servant will justify many,
and He will carry their iniquities.
[12] Therefore I will give Him the many as a portion,
and He will receive the mighty as spoil,
because He submitted Himself to death,
and was counted among the rebels;
yet He bore the sin of many
and interceded for the rebels.

## ISAIAH 54

FUTURE GLORY FOR ISRAEL

[1] "Rejoice, childless one, who did not give birth;
burst into song and shout,
you who have not been in labor!
For the children of the forsaken one will be more
than the children of the married woman,"
says the Lord.
[2] "Enlarge the site of your tent,
and let your tent curtains be stretched out;
do not hold back;
lengthen your ropes,
and drive your pegs deep.
[3] For you will spread out to the right and to the left,
and your descendants will dispossess nations
and inhabit the desolate cities.

[4] "Do not be afraid, for you will not be put to shame;
don't be humiliated, for you will not be disgraced.
For you will forget the shame of your youth,
and you will no longer remember
the disgrace of your widowhood.
[5] Indeed, your husband is your Maker—
His name is Yahweh of Hosts—
and the Holy One of Israel is your Redeemer;
He is called the God of all the earth.
[6] For the Lord has called you,

like a wife deserted and wounded in spirit,
a wife of one's youth when she is rejected,"
says your God.
[7] "I deserted you for a brief moment,
but I will take you back with great compassion.
[8] In a surge of anger
I hid My face from you for a moment,
but I will have compassion on you
with everlasting love,"
says the Lord your Redeemer.
[9] "For this is like the days of Noah to Me:
when I swore that the waters of Noah
would never flood the earth again,
so I have sworn that I will not be angry with you
or rebuke you.
[10] Though the mountains move
and the hills shake,
My love will not be removed from you
and My covenant of peace will not be shaken,"
says your compassionate Lord.

**MY LOVE will not be removed FROM YOU**

[11] "Poor Jerusalem, storm-tossed, and not comforted,
I will set your stones in black mortar,
and lay your foundations in sapphires.
[12] I will make your fortifications out of rubies,
your gates out of sparkling stones,
and all your walls out of precious stones.
[13] Then all your children will be taught by the Lord,
their prosperity will be great,
[14] and you will be established
on a foundation of righteousness.
You will be far from oppression,
you will certainly not be afraid;
you will be far from terror,
it will certainly not come near you.

<sup>15</sup> If anyone attacks you,

it is not from Me;

whoever attacks you

will fall before you.

<sup>16</sup> Look, I have created the craftsman

who blows on the charcoal fire

and produces a weapon suitable for its task;

and I have created the destroyer to cause havoc.

<sup>17</sup> No weapon formed against you will succeed,

and you will refute any accusation

raised against you in court.

This is the heritage of the Lord's servants,

and their righteousness is from Me."

This is the Lord's declaration.

## MATTHEW 8:14-17

### HEALINGS AT CAPERNAUM

<sup>14</sup> When Jesus went into Peter's house, He saw his mother-in-law lying in bed with a fever. <sup>15</sup> So He touched her hand, and the fever left her. Then she got up and began to serve Him. <sup>16</sup> When evening came, they brought to Him many who were demon-possessed. He drove out the spirits with a word and healed all who were sick, <sup>17</sup> so that what was spoken through the prophet Isaiah might be fulfilled:

He Himself took our weaknesses

and carried our diseases.

## ROMANS 3:21-26

### GOD'S RIGHTEOUSNESS THROUGH FAITH

<sup>21</sup> But now, apart from the law, God's righteousness has been revealed—attested by the Law and the Prophets <sup>22</sup> —that is, God's righteousness through faith in Jesus Christ, to all who believe, since there is no distinction. <sup>23</sup> For all have sinned and fall short of the glory of God. <sup>24</sup> They are justified freely by His grace through the redemption that is in Christ Jesus. <sup>25</sup> God presented Him as a propitiation through faith in His blood, to demonstrate His righteousness, because in His restraint God passed over the sins previously committed. <sup>26</sup> God presented Him to demonstrate His righteousness at the present time, so that He would be righteous and declare righteous the one who has faith in Jesus.

NOTES

DATE      /      /

# 39

## Come to the Lord

ISAIAH 55

COME TO THE LORD

¹ "Come, everyone who is thirsty,
come to the waters;
and you without money,
come, buy, and eat!
Come, buy wine and milk
without money and without cost!
² Why do you spend money on what is not food,
and your wages on what does not satisfy?
Listen carefully to Me, and eat what is good,
and you will enjoy the choicest of foods.
³ Pay attention and come to Me;
listen, so that you will live.
I will make an everlasting covenant with you,
the promises assured to David.
⁴ Since I have made him a witness to the peoples,
a leader and commander for the peoples,
⁵ so you will summon a nation you do not know,
and nations who do not know you will run to you.
For the Lord your God,
even the Holy One of Israel,
has glorified you."

⁶ *Seek the Lord while He may be found;
call to Him while He is near.*

⁷ Let the wicked one abandon his way
and the sinful one his thoughts;
let him return to the Lord,
so He may have compassion on him,
and to our God, for He will freely forgive.

⁸ "For My thoughts are not your thoughts,
and your ways are not My ways."

This is the Lord's declaration.

⁹ "For as heaven is higher than earth,
so My ways are higher than your ways,
and My thoughts than your thoughts.
¹⁰ For just as rain and snow fall from heaven
and do not return there
without saturating the earth

and making it germinate and sprout,
and providing seed to sow
and food to eat,
[11] so My word that comes from My mouth
will not return to Me empty,
but it will accomplish what I please
and will prosper in what I send it to do."

[12] You will indeed go out with joy
and be peacefully guided;
the mountains and the hills will break into singing
before you,
and all the trees of the field will clap their hands.
[13] Instead of the thornbush, a cypress will come up,
and instead of the brier, a myrtle will come up;
it will make a name for Yahweh
as an everlasting sign that will not be destroyed.

## ISAIAH 56

A HOUSE OF PRAYER FOR ALL

[1] This is what the Lord says:

Preserve justice and do what is right,
for My salvation is coming soon,
and My righteousness will be revealed.
[2] Happy is the man who does this,
anyone who maintains this,
who keeps the Sabbath without desecrating it,
and keeps his hand from doing any evil.

[3] No foreigner who has joined himself to the Lord
should say,
"The Lord will exclude me from His people";
and the eunuch should not say,
"Look, I am a dried-up tree."
[4] For the Lord says this:
"For the eunuchs who keep My Sabbaths,
and choose what pleases Me,
and hold firmly to My covenant,
[5] I will give them, in My house and within My walls,
a memorial and a name

better than sons and daughters.
I will give each of them an everlasting name
that will never be cut off.
[6] And the foreigners who join themselves to the Lord
minister to Him, love the name of Yahweh
and become His servants,
all who keep the Sabbath without desecrating it
and who hold firmly to My covenant—
[7] I will bring them to My holy mountain
and let them rejoice in My house of prayer.
Their burnt offerings and sacrifices
will be acceptable on My altar,
for My house will be called a house of prayer
for all nations."

*[8] This is the declaration of the Lord God,
who gathers the dispersed of Israel:*

*"I will gather to them still others
besides those already gathered."*

UNRIGHTEOUS LEADERS CONDEMNED

[9] All you animals of the field and forest,
come and eat!
[10] Israel's watchmen are blind, all of them,
they know nothing;
all of them are mute dogs,
they cannot bark;
they dream, lie down,
and love to sleep.
[11] These dogs have fierce appetites;
they never have enough.
And they are shepherds
who have no discernment;
all of them turn to their own way,
every last one for his own gain.
[12] "Come, let me get some wine,
let's guzzle some beer;
and tomorrow will be like today,
only far better!"

## JOHN 7:37-39

THE PROMISE OF THE SPIRIT

[37] On the last and most important day of the festival, Jesus stood up and cried out,

*"If anyone is thirsty, he should come to Me and drink!*
[38] *The one who believes in Me, as the Scripture has said, will have streams of living water flow from deep within him."*

[39] He said this about the Spirit. Those who believed in Jesus were going to receive the Spirit, for the Spirit had not yet been received because Jesus had not yet been glorified.

## 1 CORINTHIANS 2:9

But as it is written:

> What eye did not see and ear did not hear,
> and what never entered the human mind—
> God prepared this for those who love Him.

NOTES

DATE  /    /

# 40

## Healing and Peace

[1] The righteous one perishes,
and no one takes it to heart;
faithful men are swept away,
with no one realizing
that the righteous one is swept away
from the presence of evil.
[2] He will enter into peace—
they will rest on their beds—
everyone who lives uprightly.

### PAGAN RELIGION DENOUNCED

[3] But come here,
you sons of a sorceress,
offspring of an adulterer and a prostitute!
[4] Who is it you are mocking?
Who is it you are opening your mouth
and sticking out your tongue at?
Isn't it you, you rebellious children,
you race of liars,
[5] who burn with lust among the oaks,
under every green tree,
who slaughter children in the wadis
below the clefts of the rocks?
[6] Your portion is among the smooth stones of the wadi;
indeed, they are your lot.
You have even poured out a drink offering to them;
you have offered a grain offering;
should I be satisfied with these?
[7] You have placed your bed
on a high and lofty mountain;
you also went up there to offer sacrifice.
[8] You have set up your memorial
behind the door and doorpost.
For away from Me, you stripped,
went up, and made your bed wide,
and you have made a bargain for yourself with them.
You have loved their bed;
you have gazed on their genitals.
[9] You went to the king with oil
and multiplied your perfumes;

you sent your couriers far away

and sent them down even to Sheol.

¹⁰ You became weary on your many journeys,

but you did not say, "I give up!"

You found a renewal of your strength;

therefore you did not grow weak.

¹¹ Who was it you dreaded and feared,

so that you lied and didn't remember Me

or take it to heart?

Have I not kept silent for such a long time

and you do not fear Me?

¹² I will expose your righteousness,

and your works—they will not profit you.

¹³ When you cry out,

let your collection of idols deliver you!

The wind will carry all of them off,

a breath will take them away.

But whoever takes refuge in Me

will inherit the land

and possess My holy mountain.

HEALING AND PEACE

¹⁴ He said,

"Build it up, build it up, prepare the way,

remove every obstacle from My people's way."

¹⁵ For the High and Exalted One

who lives forever, whose name is Holy says this:

"I live in a high and holy place,

and with the oppressed and lowly of spirit,

to revive the spirit of the lowly

and revive the heart of the oppressed.

¹⁶ For I will not accuse you forever,

and I will not always be angry;

for then the spirit would grow weak before Me,

even the breath of man, which I have made.

¹⁷ Because of his sinful greed I was angry,

so I struck him; I was angry and hid;

but he went on turning back to the desires of his heart.

¹⁸ I have seen his ways, but I will heal him;

I will lead him and restore comfort

to him and his mourners,

¹⁹ creating words of praise."

The Lord says,

"Peace, peace to the one who is far or near,

and I will heal him.

²⁰ But the wicked are like the storm-tossed sea,

for it cannot be still,

and its waters churn up mire and muck.

²¹ *There is no peace for the wicked,"*
*says my God.*

**EPHESIANS 2:11-22**

UNITY IN CHRIST

¹¹ So then, remember that at one time you were Gentiles in the flesh—called "the uncircumcised" by those called "the circumcised," which is done in the flesh by human hands. ¹² At that time you were without the Messiah, excluded from the citizenship of Israel, and foreigners to the covenants of the promise, without hope and without God in the world. ¹³ But now in Christ Jesus, you who were far away have been brought near by the blood of the Messiah. ¹⁴ For He is our peace, who made both groups one and tore down the dividing wall of hostility. In His flesh, ¹⁵ He made of no effect the law consisting of commands and expressed in regulations, so that He might create in Himself one new man from the two, resulting in peace. ¹⁶ He did this so that He might reconcile both to God in one body through the cross and put the hostility to death by it. ¹⁷ When the Messiah came, He proclaimed the good news of peace to you who were far away and peace to those who were near. ¹⁸ For through Him we both have access by one Spirit to the Father. ¹⁹ So then you are no longer foreigners and strangers, but fellow citizens with the saints, and members of God's household, ²⁰ built on the foundation of the apostles and prophets, with Christ Jesus Himself as the cornerstone. ²¹ The whole building, being put together by Him, grows into a holy sanctuary in the Lord. ²² You also are being built together for God's dwelling in the Spirit.

## LUKE 12:4-7

FEAR GOD

[4] "And I say to you, My friends, don't fear those who kill the body, and after that can do nothing more. [5] But I will show you the One to fear: Fear Him who has authority to throw people into hell after death. Yes, I say to you, this is the One to fear! [6] Aren't five sparrows sold for two pennies? Yet not one of them is forgotten in God's sight. [7] Indeed, the hairs of your head are all counted. Don't be afraid; you are worth more than many sparrows!"

NOTES

DATE / /

*DAY* **41**

# GRACE
## *day*

Take this day as an opportunity to catch up on your reading, pray, and rest in the presence of the Lord.

*Don't be afraid;*
*you are worth more*
*than many sparrows!*

LUKE 12:7

MAKES *1 dozen*

# LUSCIOUS LEMON BARS

## CRUST INGREDIENTS:

½ cup finely ground raw sunflower seeds, sifted (60g)
½ cup coconut flour, sifted (90g)
½ teaspoon baking soda
2 tablespoons unsalted butter or coconut oil,
   plus more for greasing dish
2 tablespoons honey
2 eggs
1 teaspoon vanilla extract
1½ teaspoons fresh lemon juice

## FILLING:

3 large eggs plus 1 yolk, lightly beaten
½ cup honey
¾ cup fresh lemon juice, strained
3 tablespoons coconut flour, sifted
1 teaspoon lemon zest, finely grated

## INSTRUCTIONS:

Preheat oven to 350°F.

Combine all of the crust ingredients in a food processor. Process for 15 seconds to combine. Scrape down sides if necessary, and pulse once or twice more until a dough forms.

Lightly grease a 9×9 square baking dish with butter. Press the dough into the bottom and slightly up the sides of the dish.

Prick the dough a few times all over with a fork, then bake for 10 minutes. Remove from the oven and cool on a wire rack while you prepare the filling.

Whisk together all of the filling ingredients. Allow the coconut flour to absorb for 10 minutes, then whisk again until the filling is smooth. If there are any lumps of coconut flour, pass it through a mesh strainer.

Pour the filling on top of the baked crust, and bake again for 15-20 minutes or until the center is set but slightly jiggly.

Cool on a wire rack for 20 minutes, then refrigerate until chilled.

# Introduction to Holy Week

/ *WEEK SEVEN*

**If you grew up with Bible stories, you know the challenge it is to read a familiar passage of Scripture with fresh eyes. When we come to a story like the Good Samaritan or Noah and the flood, our task, as Bible scholar Kenneth Bailey used to say, is to "rescue truth from the jaws of familiarity."**

**So it is with the Easter story.** Most everyone knows Jesus died on the cross. It is one of those facts essential to the story, like how we know the Titanic sank or that Lincoln was shot in a theater. But the story of Jesus' life, death, and resurrection is drenched in details of remarkably significant insight which affect not only what we understand about the story, but also about Jesus Himself.

How clear are you on the foundational story of Jesus' death and resurrection? If you are a Christian, your confession is that Jesus died in your place and paid for your sins with His death. But why was He crucified? Was He a martyr? How secure did He make your salvation?

Prior to His arrest, Jesus said, "No one takes [My life] from Me, but I lay it down on My own. I have the right to lay it down, and I have the right to take it up again" (John 10:18). This was not simply a passing statement. It was a promise that Jesus was going to the cross on purpose.

During this last week of Lent, as we make our way through the final chapters of Isaiah, our supplemental readings will trace, in real time, the path Jesus walked that last week of His earthly ministry. On Monday, we will read what happened on the Monday before the Resurrection, on Tuesday we will read what happened on Tuesday of that week, and so on.

Our hope as we read these scriptures is that we would know Christ better through the careful study of His Word, and that we would understand that His death and resurrection were purposefully endured for our salvation. His victory over death frees us to serve Him with vigor in this life, secure in the salvation He has accomplished.

As you read, see how He laid His life down. He did this for you. 📖

# 42

## *Palm Sunday*

### MATTHEW 21:1-11

#### THE TRIUMPHAL ENTRY

¹ When they approached Jerusalem and came to Bethphage at the Mount of Olives, Jesus then sent two disciples, ² telling them, "Go into the village ahead of you. At once you will find a donkey tied there, and a colt with her. Untie them and bring them to Me. ³ If anyone says anything to you, you should say that the Lord needs them, and immediately he will send them."

⁴ This took place so that what was spoken through the prophet might be fulfilled:

⁵ Tell Daughter Zion,
"Look, your King is coming to you,
gentle, and mounted on a donkey,
even on a colt,
the foal of a beast of burden."

⁶ The disciples went and did just as Jesus directed them. ⁷ They brought the donkey and the colt; then they laid their robes on them, and He sat on them. ⁸ A very large crowd spread their robes on the road; others were cutting branches from the trees and spreading them on the road. ⁹ Then the crowds who went ahead of Him and those who followed kept shouting:

Hosanna to the Son of David!
He who comes in the name
of the Lord is the blessed One!
Hosanna in the highest heaven!

¹⁰ When He entered Jerusalem, the whole city was shaken, saying, "Who is this?" ¹¹ And the crowds kept saying, "This is the prophet Jesus from Nazareth in Galilee!"

*Emily Jeffords, Find A Sunnier Place, 2014, oil, 24x36, Private Collection*

HOLY WEEK                    / WEEK SEVEN

# 43

## Sin and Redemption

## ISAIAH 58

TRUE FASTING

[1] "Cry out loudly, don't hold back!
Raise your voice like a trumpet.
Tell My people their transgression
and the house of Jacob their sins.
[2] They seek Me day after day
and delight to know My ways,
like a nation that does what is right
and does not abandon the justice of their God.
They ask Me for righteous judgments;
they delight in the nearness of God."
[3] "Why have we fasted,
but You have not seen?
We have denied ourselves,
but You haven't noticed!"
"Look, you do as you please
on the day of your fast,
and oppress all your workers.
[4] You fast with contention and strife
to strike viciously with your fist.
You cannot fast as you do today,
hoping to make your voice heard on high.
[5] Will the fast I choose be like this:
A day for a person to deny himself,
to bow his head like a reed,
and to spread out sackcloth and ashes?
Will you call this a fast
and a day acceptable to the Lord?
[6] Isn't the fast I choose:
To break the chains of wickedness,
to untie the ropes of the yoke,
to set the oppressed free,
and to tear off every yoke?
[7] Is it not to share your bread with the hungry,
to bring the poor and homeless into your house,
to clothe the naked when you see him,
and not to ignore your own flesh and blood?
[8] Then your light will appear like the dawn,
and your recovery will come quickly.
Your righteousness will go before you,
and the Lord's glory will be your rear guard.
[9] At that time, when you call, the Lord will answer;
when you cry out, He will say, 'Here I am.'

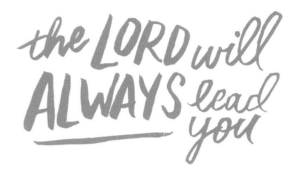

If you get rid of the yoke among you,
the finger-pointing and malicious speaking,
[10] and if you offer yourself to the hungry,
and satisfy the afflicted one,
then your light will shine in the darkness,
and your night will be like noonday.
[11] The Lord will always lead you,
satisfy you in a parched land,
and strengthen your bones.
You will be like a watered garden
and like a spring whose waters never run dry.
[12] Some of you will rebuild the ancient ruins;
you will restore the foundations laid long ago;
you will be called the repairer of broken walls,
the restorer of streets where people live.

[13] "If you keep from desecrating the Sabbath,
from doing whatever you want on My holy day;
if you call the Sabbath a delight,
and the holy day of the Lord honorable;
if you honor it, not going your own ways,
seeking your own pleasure, or talking too much;
[14] then you will delight yourself in the Lord,
and I will make you ride over the heights of the land,
and let you enjoy the heritage of your father Jacob."
For the mouth of the Lord has spoken.

## ISAIAH 59

### SIN AND REDEMPTION

¹ *Indeed, the Lord's hand is not too short*
  *to save,*
*and His ear is not too deaf to hear.*

² But your iniquities have built barriers
between you and your God,
and your sins have made Him hide His face from you
so that He does not listen.
³ For your hands are defiled with blood
and your fingers, with iniquity;
your lips have spoken lies,
and your tongues mutter injustice.
⁴ No one makes claims justly;
no one pleads honestly.
They trust in empty and worthless words;
they conceive trouble and give birth to iniquity.
⁵ They hatch viper's eggs
and weave spider's webs.
Whoever eats their eggs will die;
crack one open, and a viper is hatched.
⁶ Their webs cannot become clothing,
and they cannot cover themselves with their works.
Their works are sinful works,
and violent acts are in their hands.
⁷ Their feet run after evil,
and they rush to shed innocent blood.
Their thoughts are sinful thoughts;
ruin and wretchedness are in their paths.
⁸ They have not known the path of peace,
and there is no justice in their ways.
They have made their roads crooked;
no one who walks on them will know peace.

⁹ Therefore justice is far from us,
and righteousness does not reach us.
We hope for light, but there is darkness;
for brightness, but we live in the night.
¹⁰ We grope along a wall like the blind;
we grope like those without eyes.
We stumble at noon as though it were twilight;
we are like the dead among those who are healthy.
¹¹ We all growl like bears
and moan like doves.

We hope for justice, but there is none;
for salvation, but it is far from us.
¹² For our transgressions have multiplied before You,
and our sins testify against us.
For our transgressions are with us,
and we know our iniquities:
¹³ transgression and deception against the Lord,
turning away from following our God,
speaking oppression and revolt,
conceiving and uttering lying words from the heart.
¹⁴ Justice is turned back,
and righteousness stands far off.
For truth has stumbled in the public square,
and honesty cannot enter.
¹⁵ Truth is missing,
and whoever turns from evil is plundered.

The Lord saw that there was no justice,
and He was offended.
¹⁶ He saw that there was no man—
He was amazed that there was no one interceding;
so His own arm brought salvation,
and His own righteousness supported Him.
¹⁷ He put on righteousness like a breastplate,
and a helmet of salvation on His head;
He put on garments of vengeance for clothing,
and He wrapped Himself in zeal as in a cloak.
¹⁸ So He will repay according to their deeds:
fury to His enemies,
retribution to His foes,
and He will repay the coastlands.

¹⁹ *They will fear the name of Yahweh in the west*
*and His glory in the east;*
*for He will come like a rushing stream*
*driven by the wind of the Lord.*

²⁰ "The Redeemer will come to Zion,
  and to those in Jacob who turn from transgression."
                    This is the Lord's declaration.

²¹ "As for Me, this is My covenant with them," says the Lord: "My Spirit who is on you, and My words that I have put in your mouth, will not depart from your mouth, or from the mouth of your children, or from the mouth of your children's children, from now on and forever," says the Lord.

## MATTHEW 21:12-22

CLEANSING THE TEMPLE COMPLEX

¹² Jesus went into the temple complex and drove out all those buying and selling in the temple. He overturned the money changers' tables and the chairs of those selling doves. ¹³ And He said to them, "It is written, My house will be called a house of prayer. But you are making it a den of thieves!"

CHILDREN PRAISE JESUS

¹⁴ The blind and the lame came to Him in the temple complex, and He healed them. ¹⁵ When the chief priests and the scribes saw the wonders that He did and the children shouting in the temple complex, "Hosanna to the Son of David!" they were indignant ¹⁶ and said to Him, "Do You hear what these children are saying?"

"Yes," Jesus told them. "Have you never read:

You have prepared praise
from the mouths of children and nursing infants?"

¹⁷ Then He left them, went out of the city to Bethany, and spent the night there.

THE BARREN FIG TREE

¹⁸ Early in the morning, as He was returning to the city, He was hungry. ¹⁹ Seeing a lone fig tree by the road, He went up to it and found nothing on it except leaves. And He said to it, "May no fruit ever come from you again!" At once the fig tree withered.

²⁰ When the disciples saw it, they were amazed and said, "How did the fig tree wither so quickly?"

²¹ Jesus answered them, "I assure you: If you have faith and do not doubt, you will not only do what was done to the fig tree, but even if you tell this mountain, 'Be lifted up and thrown into the sea,' it will be done. ²² And if you believe, you will receive whatever you ask for in prayer."

HOLY WEEK                                    / *WEEK SEVEN*

*The Glory of the Lord*

## ISAIAH 60

[1] Arise, shine, for your light has come,
and the glory of the Lord shines over you.
[2] For look, darkness covers the earth,
and total darkness the peoples;
but the Lord will shine over you,
and His glory will appear over you.

[3] *Nations will come to your light,*
*and kings to the brightness of your radiance.*

[4] Raise your eyes and look around:
they all gather and come to you;
your sons will come from far away,
and your daughters will be carried on the hip.
[5] Then you will see and be radiant,
and your heart will tremble and rejoice,
because the riches of the sea will become yours
and the wealth of the nations will come to you.
[6] Caravans of camels will cover your land—
young camels of Midian and Ephah—
all of them will come from Sheba.
They will carry gold and frankincense
and proclaim the praises of the Lord.
[7] All the flocks of Kedar will be gathered to you;
the rams of Nebaioth will serve you
and go up on My altar as an acceptable sacrifice.
I will glorify My beautiful house.

[8] Who are these who fly like a cloud,
like doves to their shelters?
[9] Yes, the islands will wait for Me
with the ships of Tarshish in the lead,
to bring your children from far away,
their silver and gold with them,
for the honor of the Lord your God,
the Holy One of Israel,
who has glorified you.
[10] Foreigners will build up your walls,
and their kings will serve you.
Although I struck you in My wrath,
yet I will show mercy to you with My favor.
[11] Your gates will always be open;
they will never be shut day or night

so that the wealth of the nations
may be brought into you,
with their kings being led in procession.
[12] For the nation and the kingdom
that will not serve you will perish;
those nations will be annihilated.
[13] The glory of Lebanon will come to you—
its pine, fir, and cypress together—
to beautify the place of My sanctuary,
and I will glorify My dwelling place.
[14] The sons of your oppressors
will come and bow down to you;
all who reviled you
will fall facedown at your feet.
They will call you the City of the Lord,
Zion of the Holy One of Israel.
[15] Instead of your being deserted and hated,
with no one passing through,
I will make you an object of eternal pride,
a joy from age to age.
[16] You will nurse on the milk of nations,
and nurse at the breast of kings;
you will know that I, Yahweh, am your Savior
and Redeemer, the Mighty One of Jacob.

[17] I will bring gold instead of bronze;
I will bring silver instead of iron,
bronze instead of wood,
and iron instead of stones.
I will appoint peace as your guard
and righteousness as your ruler.
[18] Violence will never again be heard of in your land;
devastation and destruction
will be gone from your borders.
But you will name your walls salvation
and your gates, praise.
[19] The sun will no longer be your light by day,
and the brightness of the moon will not shine on you;
but the Lord will be your everlasting light,
and your God will be your splendor.
[20] Your sun will no longer set,
and your moon will not fade;
for the Lord will be your everlasting light,
and the days of your sorrow will be over.

²¹ Then all your people will be righteous;
they will possess the land forever;
they are the branch I planted,
the work of My hands,
so that I may be glorified.
²² The least will become a thousand,
the smallest a mighty nation.
I am Yahweh;
I will accomplish it quickly in its time.

## ISAIAH 61

MESSIAH'S JUBILEE

¹ The Spirit of the Lord God is on Me,
because the Lord has anointed Me
to bring good news to the poor.
He has sent Me to heal the brokenhearted,
to proclaim liberty to the captives
and freedom to the prisoners;
² to proclaim the year of the Lord's favor,
and the day of our God's vengeance;
to comfort all who mourn,
³ to provide for those who mourn in Zion;
to give them a crown of beauty instead of ashes,
festive oil instead of mourning,
and splendid clothes instead of despair.
And they will be called righteous trees,
planted by the Lord
to glorify Him.

⁴ They will rebuild the ancient ruins;
they will restore the former devastations;

they will renew the ruined cities,
the devastations of many generations.
⁵ Strangers will stand and feed your flocks,
and foreigners will be your plowmen and vinedressers.
⁶ But you will be called the Lord's priests;
they will speak of you as ministers of our God;
you will eat the wealth of the nations,
and you will boast in their riches.
⁷ Because your shame was double,
and they cried out, "Disgrace is their portion,"
therefore, they will possess double in their land,
and eternal joy will be theirs.

⁸ For I Yahweh love justice;
I hate robbery and injustice;
I will faithfully reward them
and make an everlasting covenant with them.
⁹ Their descendants will be known among the nations,
and their posterity among the peoples.
All who see them will recognize
that they are a people the Lord has blessed.

¹⁰ I greatly rejoice in the Lord,
I exult in my God;
for He has clothed me with the garments of salvation
and wrapped me in a robe of righteousness,
as a groom wears a turban
and as a bride adorns herself with her jewels.
¹¹ For as the earth produces its growth,
and as a garden enables what is sown to spring up,
so the Lord God will cause righteousness and praise
to spring up before all the nations.

## MATTHEW 25:31-46

THE SHEEP AND THE GOATS

³¹ "When the Son of Man comes in His glory, and all the angels with Him, then He will sit on the throne of His glory. ³² All the nations will be gathered before Him, and He will separate them one from another, just as a shepherd separates the sheep from the goats. ³³ He will put the sheep on His right and the goats on the left. ³⁴ Then the King will say to those on His right, 'Come, you who are blessed by My Father, inherit the kingdom prepared for you from the foundation of the world.

<sup>35</sup> For I was hungry
and you gave Me something to eat;
I was thirsty
and you gave Me something to drink;
I was a stranger and you took Me in;
<sup>36</sup> I was naked and you clothed Me;
I was sick and you took care of Me;
I was in prison and you visited Me.'

<sup>37</sup> "Then the righteous will answer Him, 'Lord, when did we see You hungry and feed You, or thirsty and give You something to drink? <sup>38</sup> When did we see You a stranger and take You in, or without clothes and clothe You? <sup>39</sup> When did we see You sick, or in prison, and visit You?'

<sup>40</sup> "And the King will answer them, 'I assure you: Whatever you did for one of the least of these brothers of Mine, you did for Me.' <sup>41</sup> Then He will also say to those on the left, 'Depart from Me, you who are cursed, into the eternal fire prepared for the Devil and his angels!

<sup>42</sup> For I was hungry
and you gave Me nothing to eat;
I was thirsty
and you gave Me nothing to drink;
<sup>43</sup> I was a stranger
and you didn't take Me in;
I was naked
and you didn't clothe Me,
sick and in prison
and you didn't take care of Me.'

<sup>44</sup> "Then they too will answer, 'Lord, when did we see You hungry, or thirsty, or a stranger, or without clothes, or sick, or in prison, and not help You?'

<sup>45</sup> "Then He will answer them, 'I assure you: Whatever you did not do for one of the least of these, you did not do for Me either.'

<sup>46</sup> "And they will go away into eternal punishment, but the righteous into eternal life."

# 45

## *Restoration*

## ISAIAH 62

ZION'S RESTORATION

¹ I will not keep silent because of Zion,
and I will not keep still because of Jerusalem,
until her righteousness shines like a bright light
and her salvation, like a flaming torch.
² Nations will see your righteousness
and all kings, your glory.
You will be called by a new name
that the Lord's mouth will announce.
³ You will be a glorious crown in the Lord's hand,
and a royal diadem in the palm of your God.
⁴ You will no longer be called Deserted,
and your land will not be called Desolate;
instead, you will be called My Delight is in Her,
and your land Married;
for the Lord delights in you,
and your land will be married.
⁵ For as a young man marries a young woman,
so your sons will marry you;

*and as a groom rejoices over his bride,
so your God will rejoice over you.*

⁶ Jerusalem,
I have appointed watchmen on your walls;
they will never be silent, day or night.
There is no rest for you,
who remind the Lord.
⁷ Do not give Him rest
until He establishes and makes Jerusalem
the praise of the earth.

⁸ The Lord has sworn with His right hand
and His strong arm:
I will no longer give your grain
to your enemies for food,
and foreigners will not drink your new wine
you have labored for.
⁹ For those who gather grain will eat it
and praise the Lord,
and those who harvest the grapes will drink the wine
in My holy courts.

¹⁰ Go out, go out through the gates;
prepare a way for the people!
Build it up, build up the highway;
clear away the stones!
Raise a banner for the peoples.
¹¹ Look, the Lord has proclaimed
to the ends of the earth,
"Say to Daughter Zion:
Look, your salvation is coming,
His reward is with Him,
and His gifts accompany Him."
¹² And they will be called the Holy People,
the Lord's Redeemed;
and you will be called Cared For,
A City Not Deserted.

## ISAIAH 63:1-14

THE LORD'S DAY OF VENGEANCE

¹ Who is this coming from Edom
in crimson-stained garments from Bozrah—
this One who is splendid in His apparel,
rising up proudly in His great might?

It is I, proclaiming vindication,
powerful to save.

² Why are Your clothes red,
and Your garments like one who treads a winepress?

³ I trampled the winepress alone,
and no one from the nations was with Me.
I trampled them in My anger
and ground them underfoot in My fury;
their blood spattered My garments,
and all My clothes were stained.
⁴ For I planned the day of vengeance,
and the year of My redemption came.
⁵ I looked, but there was no one to help,
and I was amazed that no one assisted;
so My arm accomplished victory for Me,
and My wrath assisted Me.
⁶ I crushed nations in My anger;
I made them drunk with My wrath
and poured out their blood on the ground.

⁷ I will make known the Lord's faithful love
and the Lord's praiseworthy acts,
because of all the Lord has done for us—
even the many good things
He has done for the house of Israel
and has done for them based on His compassion
and the abundance of His faithful love.
⁸ He said, "They are indeed My people,
children who will not be disloyal,"
and He became their Savior.
⁹ In all their suffering, He suffered,
and the Angel of His Presence saved them.
He redeemed them
because of His love and compassion;
He lifted them up and carried them
all the days of the past.
¹⁰ But they rebelled
and grieved His Holy Spirit.
So He became their enemy
and fought against them.
¹¹ Then He remembered the days of the past,
the days of Moses and his people.
Where is He who brought them out of the sea
with the shepherds of His flock?
Where is He who put His Holy Spirit among the flock?
¹² He sent His glorious arm
to be at Moses' right hand,
divided the waters before them
to obtain eternal fame for Himself,
¹³ and led them through the depths
like a horse in the wilderness,
so that they did not stumble.
¹⁴ Like cattle that go down into the valley,
the Spirit of the Lord gave them rest.
You led Your people this way
to make a glorious name for Yourself.

## MATTHEW 26:1-16

### THE PLOT TO KILL JESUS

¹ When Jesus had finished saying all this, He told His disciples, ² "You know that the Passover takes place after two days, and the Son of Man will be handed over to be crucified."

³ Then the chief priests and the elders of the people assembled in the palace of the high priest, who was called Caiaphas, ⁴ and they conspired to arrest Jesus in a treacherous way and kill Him. ⁵ "Not during the festival," they said, "so there won't be rioting among the people."

### THE ANOINTING AT BETHANY

⁶ While Jesus was in Bethany at the house of Simon, a man who had a serious skin disease, ⁷ a woman approached Him with an alabaster jar of very expensive fragrant oil. She poured it on His head as He was reclining at the table. ⁸ When the disciples saw it, they were indignant. "Why this waste?" they asked. ⁹ "This might have been sold for a great deal and given to the poor."

¹⁰ But Jesus, aware of this, said to them, "Why are you bothering this woman? She has done a noble thing for Me. ¹¹ You always have the poor with you, but you do not always have Me. ¹² By pouring this fragrant oil on My body, she has prepared Me for burial. ¹³ I assure you: Wherever this gospel is proclaimed in the whole world, what this woman has done will also be told in memory of her."

¹⁴ Then one of the Twelve—the man called Judas Iscariot—went to the chief priests ¹⁵ and said, "What are you willing to give me if I hand Him over to you?" So they weighed out 30 pieces of silver for him. ¹⁶ And from that time he started looking for a good opportunity to betray Him.

NOTES

DATE      /      /

HOLY WEEK                    / *WEEK SEVEN*

# 46

*A New Creation*

## ISAIAH 63:15-19

ISRAEL'S PRAYER

[15] Look down from heaven and see
from Your lofty home—holy and beautiful.
Where is Your zeal and Your might?
Your yearning and Your compassion
are withheld from me.
[16] Yet You are our Father,
even though Abraham does not know us
and Israel doesn't recognize us.
You, Yahweh, are our Father;
from ancient times,
Your name is our Redeemer.
[17] Why, Yahweh, do You make us stray from Your ways?
You harden our hearts so we do not fear You.
Return, because of Your servants,
the tribes of Your heritage.
[18] Your holy people had a possession
for a little while,
but our enemies have trampled down
Your sanctuary.
[19] We have become like those You never ruled over,
like those not called by Your name.

YOUR name is our REDEEMER.

## ISAIAH 64

[1] If only You would tear the heavens open
and come down,
so that mountains would quake at Your presence—
[2] as fire kindles the brushwood,
and fire causes water to boil—
to make Your name known to Your enemies,
so that nations will tremble at Your presence!
[3] When You did awesome works
that we did not expect,
You came down,
and the mountains quaked at Your presence.
[4] From ancient times no one has heard,
no one has listened,
no eye has seen any God except You,
who acts on behalf of the one who waits for Him.
[5] You welcome the one who joyfully does what is right;
they remember You in Your ways.
But we have sinned, and You were angry.
How can we be saved if we remain in our sins?

[6] All of us have become like something unclean,
and all our righteous acts are like a polluted garment;
all of us wither like a leaf,
and our iniquities carry us away like the wind.
[7] No one calls on Your name,
striving to take hold of You.
For You have hidden Your face from us
and made us melt because of our iniquity.

[8] Yet Lord, You are our Father;
we are the clay, and You are our potter;
we all are the work of Your hands.
[9] Lord, do not be terribly angry
or remember our iniquity forever.
Please look—all of us are Your people!
[10] Your holy cities have become a wilderness;
Zion has become a wilderness,
Jerusalem a desolation.
[11] Our holy and beautiful temple,
where our fathers praised You,
has been burned with fire,
and all that was dear to us lies in ruins.
[12] Lord, after all this, will You restrain Yourself?
Will You keep silent and afflict severely?

**ISAIAH 65**

THE LORD'S RESPONSE

¹ "I was sought by those who did not ask;
I was found by those who did not seek Me.
I said: Here I am, here I am,
to a nation that was not called by My name.
² I spread out My hands all day long
to a rebellious people
who walk in the wrong path,
following their own thoughts.
³ These people continually provoke Me
to My face,
sacrificing in gardens,
burning incense on bricks,
⁴ sitting among the graves,
spending nights in secret places,
eating the meat of pigs,
and putting polluted broth in their bowls.
⁵ They say, 'Keep to yourself,
don't come near me, for I am too holy for you!'
These practices are smoke in My nostrils,
a fire that burns all day long.
⁶ It is written before Me:
I will not keep silent, but I will repay;
I will repay them fully
⁷ for your iniquities and the iniquities
of your fathers together,"
says the Lord.
"Because they burned incense on the mountains
and reproached Me on the hills,
I will reward them fully
for their former deeds."

⁸ The Lord says this:

As the new wine is found in a bunch of grapes,
and one says, 'Don't destroy it,
for there's some good in it,'
so I will act because of My servants
and not destroy them all.

our INIQUITIES carry us away like the WIND

⁹ I will produce descendants from Jacob,
and heirs to My mountains from Judah;
My chosen ones will possess it,
and My servants will dwell there.
¹⁰ Sharon will be a pasture for flocks,
and the Valley of Achor a place for cattle to lie down,
for My people who have sought Me.
¹¹ But you who abandon the Lord,
who forget My holy mountain,
who prepare a table for Fortune
and fill bowls of mixed wine for Destiny,
¹² I will destine you for the sword,
and all of you will kneel down to be slaughtered,
because I called and you did not answer,
I spoke and you did not hear;
you did what was evil in My sight
and chose what I did not delight in.

¹³ Therefore, this is what the Lord God says:

My servants will eat,
but you will be hungry;
My servants will drink,
but you will be thirsty;
My servants will rejoice,
but you will be put to shame.
¹⁴ My servants will shout for joy from a glad heart,
but you will cry out from an anguished heart,
and you will lament out of a broken spirit.
¹⁵ You will leave your name behind
as a curse for My chosen ones,
and the Lord God will kill you;
but He will give His servants another name.
¹⁶ Whoever is blessed in the land
will be blessed by the God of truth,
and whoever swears in the land
will swear by the God of truth.
For the former troubles will be forgotten
and hidden from My sight.

## A NEW CREATION

¹⁷ *"For I will create a new heaven
and a new earth;
the past events will not be
remembered or come to mind.*

¹⁸ Then be glad and rejoice forever
in what I am creating;
for I will create Jerusalem to be a joy
and its people to be a delight.
¹⁹ I will rejoice in Jerusalem
and be glad in My people.
The sound of weeping and crying
will no longer be heard in her.
²⁰ In her, a nursing infant will no longer live
only a few days,
or an old man not live out his days.
Indeed, the youth will die at a hundred years,
and the one who misses a hundred years will be cursed.
²¹ People will build houses and live in them;
they will plant vineyards and eat their fruit.
²² They will not build and others live in them;
they will not plant and others eat.
For My people's lives will be
like the lifetime of a tree.
My chosen ones will fully enjoy
the work of their hands.
²³ They will not labor without success
or bear children destined for disaster,
for they will be a people blessed by the Lord
along with their descendants.
²⁴ Even before they call, I will answer;
while they are still speaking, I will hear.
²⁵ The wolf and the lamb will feed together,
and the lion will eat straw like the ox,
but the serpent's food will be dust!
They will not do what is evil or destroy
on My entire holy mountain,"
says the Lord.

## MATTHEW 26:20-50

[20] When evening came, He was reclining at the table with the Twelve. [21] While they were eating, He said, "I assure you: One of you will betray Me."

[22] Deeply distressed, each one began to say to Him, "Surely not I, Lord?"

[23] He replied, "The one who dipped his hand with Me in the bowl—he will betray Me. [24] The Son of Man will go just as it is written about Him, but woe to that man by whom the Son of Man is betrayed! It would have been better for that man if he had not been born."

[25] Then Judas, His betrayer, replied, "Surely not I, Rabbi?"

"You have said it," He told him.

### THE FIRST LORD'S SUPPER

[26] As they were eating, Jesus took bread, blessed and broke it, gave it to the disciples, and said, "Take and eat it; this is My body." [27] Then He took a cup, and after giving thanks, He gave it to them and said, "Drink from it, all of you. [28] For this is My blood that establishes the covenant; it is shed for many for the forgiveness of sins. [29] But I tell you, from this moment I will not drink of this fruit of the vine until that day when I drink it in a new way in My Father's kingdom with you." [30] After singing psalms, they went out to the Mount of Olives.

### PETER'S DENIAL PREDICTED

[31] Then Jesus said to them, "Tonight all of you will run away because of Me, for it is written:

I will strike the shepherd,
and the sheep of the flock will be scattered.

[32] But after I have been resurrected, I will go ahead of you to Galilee."

[33] Peter told Him, "Even if everyone runs away because of You, I will never run away!"

[34] "I assure you," Jesus said to him, "tonight, before the rooster crows, you will deny Me three times!"

[35] "Even if I have to die with You," Peter told Him, "I will never deny You!" And all the disciples said the same thing.

### THE PRAYER IN THE GARDEN

[36] Then Jesus came with them to a place called Gethsemane, and He told the disciples, "Sit here while I go over there and pray." [37] Taking along Peter and the two sons of Zebedee, He began to be sorrowful and deeply distressed. [38] Then He said to them, "My soul is swallowed up in sorrow —to the point of death. Remain here and stay awake with Me." [39] Going a little farther, He fell facedown and prayed, "My Father! If it is possible, let this cup pass from Me. Yet not as I will, but as You will."

[40] Then He came to the disciples and found them sleeping. He asked Peter, "So, couldn't you stay awake with Me one hour? [41] Stay awake and pray, so that you won't enter into temptation. The spirit is willing, but the flesh is weak."

[42] Again, a second time, He went away and prayed, "My Father, if this cannot pass unless I drink it, Your will be done." [43] And He came again and found them sleeping, because they could not keep their eyes open.

[44] After leaving them, He went away again and prayed a third time, saying the same thing once more. [45] Then He came to the disciples and said to them, "Are you still sleeping and resting? Look, the time is near. The Son of Man is being betrayed into the hands of sinners. [46] Get up; let's go! See, My betrayer is near."

### THE JUDAS KISS

[47] While He was still speaking, Judas, one of the Twelve, suddenly arrived. A large mob, with swords and clubs, was with him from the chief priests and elders of the people. [48] His betrayer had given them a sign: "The One I kiss, He's the One; arrest Him!" [49] So he went right up to Jesus and said, "Greetings, Rabbi!" and kissed Him.

[50] "Friend," Jesus asked him, "why have you come?" Then they came up, took hold of Jesus, and arrested Him.

NOTES

DATE      /      /

# 47

## Good Friday

### ISAIAH 66

#### FINAL JUDGMENT AND JOYOUS RESTORATION

[1] This is what the Lord says:

Heaven is My throne,
and earth is My footstool.
What house could you possibly build for Me?
And what place could be My home?
[2] My hand made all these things,
and so they all came into being.
This is the Lord's declaration.
I will look favorably on this kind of person:
one who is humble, submissive in spirit,
and trembles at My word.

[3] One slaughters an ox, one kills a man;
one sacrifices a lamb, one breaks a dog's neck;
one offers a grain offering, one offers pig's blood;
one offers incense, one praises an idol—
all these have chosen their ways
and delight in their detestable practices.
[4] So I will choose their punishment,
and I will bring on them what they dread
because I called and no one answered;
I spoke and they didn't hear;
they did what was evil in My sight
and chose what I didn't delight in.

⁵ You who tremble at His word,
hear the word of the Lord:
"Your brothers who hate and exclude you
because of Me have said,
'Let the Lord be glorified
so that we can see your joy!'
But they will be put to shame."

⁶ A sound of uproar from the city!
A voice from the temple—
the voice of the Lord,
paying back His enemies what they deserve!

⁷ Before Zion was in labor, she gave birth;
before she was in pain, she delivered a boy.
⁸ Who has heard of such a thing?
Who has seen such things?
Can a land be born in one day
or a nation be delivered in an instant?
Yet as soon as Zion was in labor,
she gave birth to her sons.
⁹ "Will I bring a baby to the point of birth
and not deliver it?"
says the Lord;
"or will I who deliver, close the womb?"
says your God.

¹⁰ *Be glad for Jerusalem and rejoice*
    *over her,*
*all who love her.*

Rejoice greatly with her,
all who mourn over her—
¹¹ so that you may nurse and be satisfied
from her comforting breast
and drink deeply and delight yourselves
from her glorious breasts.

¹² For this is what the Lord says:

I will make peace flow to her like a river,
and the wealth of nations like a flood;
you will nurse and be carried on her hip
and bounced on her lap.
¹³ As a mother comforts her son,
so I will comfort you,
and you will be comforted in Jerusalem.

¹⁴ You will see, you will rejoice,
and you will flourish like grass;
then the Lord's power will be revealed to His servants,
but He will show His wrath against His enemies.
¹⁵ Look, the Lord will come with fire—
His chariots are like the whirlwind—
to execute His anger with fury
and His rebuke with flames of fire.
¹⁶ For the Lord will execute judgment
on all flesh with His fiery sword,
and many will be slain by the Lord.

¹⁷ "Those who dedicate and purify themselves to enter the groves following their leader, eating meat from pigs, vermin, and rats, will perish together."

This is the Lord's declaration.

¹⁸ "Knowing their works and their thoughts, I have come to gather all nations and languages; they will come and see My glory. ¹⁹ I will establish a sign among them, and I will send survivors from them to the nations—to Tarshish, Put, Lud (who are archers), Tubal, Javan, and the islands far away—who have not heard of My fame or seen My glory. And they will proclaim My glory among the nations. ²⁰ They will bring all your brothers from all the nations as a gift to the Lord on horses and chariots, in litters, and on mules and camels, to My holy mountain Jerusalem," says the Lord, "just as the Israelites bring an offering in a clean vessel to the house of the Lord. ²¹ I will also take some of them as priests and Levites," says the Lord.

²² "For just as the new heavens and the new earth,
which I will make,
will endure before Me"—
this is the Lord's declaration—
"so your offspring and your name will endure.
²³ All mankind will come to worship Me
from one New Moon to another
and from one Sabbath to another,"
says the Lord.

²⁴ "As they leave, they will see the dead bodies of the men who have rebelled against Me; for their worm will never die, their fire will never go out, and they will be a horror to all mankind."

## MATTHEW 27:32-50

CRUCIFIED BETWEEN TWO CRIMINALS

[32] As they were going out, they found a Cyrenian man named Simon. They forced this man to carry His cross. [33] When they came to a place called Golgotha (which means Skull Place), [34] they gave Him wine mixed with gall to drink. But when He tasted it, He would not drink it. [35] After crucifying Him they divided His clothes by casting lots. [36] Then they sat down and were guarding Him there. [37] Above His head they put up the charge against Him in writing:

THIS IS JESUS
THE KING OF THE JEWS.

[38] Then two criminals were crucified with Him, one on the right and one on the left. [39] Those who passed by were yelling insults at Him, shaking their heads [40] and saying, "The One who would demolish the sanctuary and rebuild it in three days, save Yourself! If You are the Son of God, come down from the cross!" [41] In the same way the chief priests, with the scribes and elders, mocked Him and said, [42] "He saved others, but He cannot save Himself! He is the King of Israel! Let Him come down now from the cross, and we will believe in Him. [43] He has put His trust in God; let God rescue Him now—if He wants Him! For He said, 'I am God's Son.'" [44] In the same way even the criminals who were crucified with Him kept taunting Him.

THE DEATH OF JESUS

[45] From noon until three in the afternoon darkness came over the whole land. [46] About three in the afternoon Jesus cried out with a loud voice, "Elí, Elí, lemá sabachtháni?" that is, "My God, My God, why have You forsaken Me?"

[47] When some of those standing there heard this, they said, "He's calling for Elijah!"

[48] Immediately one of them ran and got a sponge, filled it with sour wine, fixed it on a reed, and offered Him a drink. [49] But the rest said, "Let's see if Elijah comes to save Him!"

[50] Jesus shouted again with a loud voice and gave up His spirit.

NOTES

DATE      /      /

# 48

## *Holy Saturday*

### MATTHEW 27:62-66

THE CLOSELY GUARDED TOMB

[62] The next day, which followed the preparation day, the chief priests and the Pharisees gathered before Pilate [63] and said, "Sir, we remember that while this deceiver was still alive He said, 'After three days I will rise again.' [64] Therefore give orders that the tomb be made secure until the third day. Otherwise, His disciples may come, steal Him, and tell the people, 'He has been raised from the dead.' Then the last deception will be worse than the first."

[65] "You have a guard of soldiers," Pilate told them. "Go and make it as secure as you know how." [66] Then they went and made the tomb secure by sealing the stone and setting the guard.

*Emily Jeffords, Lace Bloom Afternoon No. 1, 2016, oil, 12x12, Private Collection*

**INGREDIENTS:**

4 large eggs, at room temperature
½ cup honey
¼ cup coconut oil, melted
½ teaspoon vanilla extract
½ cup coconut flour, sifted
1 teaspoon baking soda
¾ teaspoon ground cinnamon
½ teaspoon ground nutmeg
¼ teaspoon ground ginger
¼ teaspoon sea salt
1¼ cups grated carrots
¼ cup chopped raisins or chopped pecans

**FROSTING:**

¼ cup coconut butter
3 tablespoons honey
1 tablespoon coconut oil, softened
1 tablespoon full-fat coconut milk
½ teaspoon fresh lemon juice
¼ teaspoon apple cider vinegar
¼ cup unsweetened shredded coconut (for garnish)

MAKES *1 dozen*

# CARROT CAKE CUPCAKES

**INSTRUCTIONS:**

Preheat the oven to 350°F and line a muffin tin with parchment paper liners.

Beat the eggs, honey, coconut oil, and vanilla in the bowl of a stand mixer on medium speed for 30 seconds, or use an electric hand mixer.

Add the coconut flour, baking soda, spices, and salt, and beat again to combine fully. Fold in the carrots and, if desired, the raisins or pecans.

Bake the cupcakes for 18 to 20 minutes, until a toothpick inserted in the center comes out clean. Remove the cupcakes from the pan and allow to cool completely on a wire rack before serving or frosting.

For the frosting, combine all of the frosting ingredients in a small food processor or in the bowl of a stand mixer and beat until smooth. If the frosting is too thin, place in the refrigerator for 10 minutes, then beat again. Top with the shredded coconut.

# 49

## *Easter Sunday*

### MATTHEW 28

RESURRECTION MORNING

[1] After the Sabbath, as the first day of the week was dawning, Mary Magdalene and the other Mary went to view the tomb. [2] Suddenly there was a violent earthquake, because an angel of the Lord descended from heaven and approached the tomb. He rolled back the stone and was sitting on it. [3] His appearance was like lightning, and his robe was as white as snow. [4] The guards were so shaken from fear of him that they became like dead men.

[5] But the angel told the women, "Don't be afraid, because I know you are looking for Jesus who was crucified. [6] He is not here! For He has been resurrected, just as He said. Come and see the place where He lay. [7] Then go quickly and tell His disciples, 'He has been raised from the dead. In fact, He is going ahead of you to Galilee; you will see Him there.' Listen, I have told you."

*Continued*

Emily Jeffords, From The Valley, 2013, oil, 16X20, Private Collection

# ALLELUIA, SING TO JESUS!

TEXT: WILLIAM DIX, 1866    TUNE: ROWLAND PRICHARD
ARR: RALPH VAUGHAN WILLIAMS

1 Al - le - lu - ia, sing to Je - sus! His the scep - ter, His the throne:
2 Al - le - lu - ia! not as or - phans are we left in sor - row now;
3 Al - le - lu - ia! hea - venly High Priest, here on earth our help, our stay;

Al - le - lu - ia! His the tri - umph, His the vic - to - ry a - lone.
Al - le - lu - ia! He is near us; faith be - lieves nor ques - tions how.
Al - le - lu - ia! hear the sin - ful cry to You from day to day.

Hark! the songs of peace - ful Zi - on thun - der like a migh - ty flood.
Though the cloud from sight re - ceived Him when the for - ty days were o'er,
In - ter - ces - sor, Friend of sin - ners, earth's Re - dee - mer, hear our plea,

Je - sus, out of e - very na - tion, has re - deemed us by His blood.
shall our hearts for - get His pro - mise, "I am with you ev - er - more"?
where the songs of all the sin - less sweep a - cross the crys - tal sea.

[8] So, departing quickly from the tomb with fear and great joy, they ran to tell His disciples the news. [9] Just then Jesus met them and said, "Good morning!"

*They came up, took hold of His feet, and worshiped Him.*

[10] Then Jesus told them, "Do not be afraid. Go and tell My brothers to leave for Galilee, and they will see Me there."

### THE SOLDIERS ARE BRIBED TO LIE

[11] As they were on their way, some of the guards came into the city and reported to the chief priests everything that had happened. [12] After the priests had assembled with the elders and agreed on a plan, they gave the soldiers a large sum of money [13] and told them, "Say this, 'His disciples came during the night and stole Him while we were sleeping.' [14] If this reaches the governor's ears, we will deal with him and keep you out of trouble." [15] So they took the money and did as they were instructed. And this story has been spread among Jewish people to this day.

### THE GREAT COMMISSION

[16] The 11 disciples traveled to Galilee, to the mountain where Jesus had directed them. [17] When they saw Him, they worshiped, but some doubted. [18] Then Jesus came near and said to them, "All authority has been given to Me in heaven and on earth. [19] Go, therefore, and make disciples of all nations, baptizing them in the name of the Father and of the Son and of the Holy Spirit, [20] teaching them to observe everything I have commanded you.

*And remember, I am with you always, to the end of the age."*

*Emily Jeffords, Morning Blooms No. 2, 2015, oil, 4X4, Private Collection*

we are an EASTER people and ALLELUIA is OUR song.

—ST. AUGUSTINE

# Where did I study?

- ○ HOME
- ○ CHURCH
- ○ A FRIEND'S HOUSE
- ○ SCHOOL
- ○ COFFEE SHOP
- ○ OTHER

DID I LISTEN TO MUSIC?

ARTIST:

SONG:

SCRIPTURE I WILL
SHARE WITH A FRIEND:

WHEN DID I HAVE MY BEST STUDYING SUCCESS?

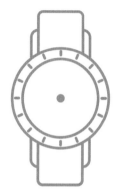

WHAT WAS HAPPENING IN THE WORLD?

# What was my best takeaway?

WHAT WAS MY BIGGEST FEAR?

▷ What was my greatest comfort?

_____

_____

_____

_____

_____

I LEARNED THESE UNEXPECTED NEW THINGS:

1

2

3

END DATE

| MONTH | DAY | YEAR |

*paintings*

# EMILY JEFFORDS

EMILY is a mixed media artist focused on creating light, nature, and peace in her work. She paints from a communal 1890's historic studio space in South Carolina, where she lives with her husband and two little girls.

**EmilyJeffords.com**
**@Emily_Jeffords**

# DANIELLE WALKER

**DANIELLE** is the author of three New York Times best-selling cookbooks: *Against All Grain, Meals Made Simple*, and *Celebrations*. After being diagnosed with an autoimmune disease and suffering for many years, Danielle found healing through dietary changes. She is a self-trained chef who tempts a range of appetites with innovative and accessible grain-free recipes on her blog, Against All Grain. She lives with her husband and two sons in the San Francisco Bay Area.

**AgainstAllGrain.com**
**@againstallgrain**

This book was printed offset in Nashville, Tennessee, on 70# Lynx Opaque. Typefaces used include Utopia, Garamond, Tribute, and Euclid. Cover is printed offset on 12 pt Saturn C1S with a soft-touch matte laminate. Finished size is 8"x10".

EDITORS-IN-CHIEF: Raechel Myers and Amanda Bible Williams

MANAGING EDITOR: Rebecca Faires

EDITORS: Russ Ramsey and Kara Gause

CREATIVE DIRECTOR: Ryan Myers

ART DIRECTOR: Amanda Barnhart

ARTWORK: Emily Jeffords

LETTERING: Naomi Scheel

DESIGNER: Kelsea Allen

THEOLOGICAL OVERSIGHT:
Russ Ramsey, MDiv., ThM.
and Nate Shurden, MDiv.

COVER ART: *Hope Rising* by Emily Jeffords

FOOD RECIPES & PHOTOGRAPHY: Danielle Walker

COMMUNITY CORRESPONDENT: Kaitlin Wernet

EDITORIAL INTERNS: Savannah Summers and Ellen Taylor

SUBSCRIPTION INQUIRIES:
orders@shereadstruth.com

She Reads Truth is a worldwide community of women who
read God's Word together every day.


Founded in 2012, She Reads Truth invites women of
all ages to engage with Scripture through daily reading
plans, online conversation led by a vibrant community of
contributors, and offline resources created at the intersection
of beauty, goodness, and Truth.

**STOP BY**

shereadstruth.com

**SHOP**

shopshereadstruth.com

**KEEP IN TOUCH**

@shereadstruth

**DOWNLOAD THE APP**

**SEND A NOTE**

hello@shereadstruth.com

**CONNECT**

#SheReadsTruth

# Beauty

We've been settling into the new **#SRThq** for the past few months—arranging our desks, organizing book shelves, meeting our mailman, and creating new routines. But the most beautiful and surprising addition to our days sits behind the parking lot and beyond the fence (just look the other way while we hop over it!). Situated right in the middle of town, it's the most glorious, wooded walking path we've ever seen. When we need an analog break or a few minutes of quiet, we slip out the back door to soak in the beauty of getting almost lost in the woods. It's just right.

# Goodness

We can't stop listening to Red Sea Road, the latest album from singer/songwriter (and fellow She!), **Ellie Holcomb**. With Scripture-rich lyrics and anthem-worthy melodies, Ellie celebrates the hope we have in Jesus, singing of the powerful and personal ways she has seen God make a way through life's toughest trials and heartache. Each song is filled with goodness for your ears and truth for your heart, but "He Will" and "Man of Sorrows" are our favorites for this Lenten season.

Last year we released our first-ever **Kids Read Truth** resource—a set of Advent Table Cards, complete with adorable illustrations and thought-provoking questions. We're thrilled to introduce an all-new set of KRT cards—just in time for Lent! We have loved hearing from our Shes and Hes about the conversations these card sets have sparked around the dinner table (or in the minivan, or on the playroom floor). One sweet mom shared that it was during a KRT-card moment that her daughter prayed to receive Christ. Praise the Lord! God is faithful.

Tell us about the conversations you're having at **hello@SheReadsTruth.com**

# & Truth